Advance Praise for *Shelf Life of a Trophy Wife*

In *Shelf Life of a Trophy Wife*, Lisa invites readers to peer beyond the glossy facade of her seemingly perfect life, revealing a deeply honest and profoundly human memoir. With Southern charm and unflinching candor, she weaves a narrative that exposes the hidden scars of abusive relationships, the haunting aftermath of suicide, and the lasting impact of sexual abuse.

What sets this memoir apart is its balance of raw vulnerability and unexpected humor. Lisa's voice is as warm as it is incisive, wrapping the reader in her world of designer clothes and high society while steadily pulling back the curtain to show the struggles and resilience that define her journey. Her ability to infuse even the darkest chapters with wit and charm is nothing short of remarkable. This is not just a story of survival but a testament to the power of authenticity. Lisa's narrative will resonate with anyone who has ever hidden their pain beneath a polished exterior. It's a poignant reminder that strength is found not in perfection but in the courage to confront the truth. *Shelf Life of a Trophy Wife* is a compelling, heartbreaking, and ultimately uplifting memoir that stays with you long after the final page.

Elissa Rosen
Lifestyle Journalist, Freelance Reporter **PEOPLE** magazine

In *Shelf Life of a Trophy Wife*, author Lisa Rayner delivers a sharp, hilarious, and deeply troubling portrait of Southern high society's rules—and the unspoken costs of fitting in. Lisa has the kind of life her mother always dreamed of: stunning homes; three rich ex-husbands, and a solid spot among the black-tie gala beau monde. But after stumbling again and again over her husbands' hidden faults—she realizes her picture-perfect world may be nothing more than a beautiful illusion. And it may all be tied to her troubling secrets from childhood. Set against the lush, genteel landscapes of Georgia, Rayner's novel peels back the layers of Southern charm to reveal the insecurities, rivalries and resilience of women who've been told who and what to be. *Shelf Life of a Trophy Wife* is a bold, unforgettable story about rediscovering one's self and finding the steel magnolia within. This thought-provoking memoir will leave readers questioning what "having it all" really means.

Stephanie Davis Smith
Former editor at **GQ, Self, The Atlantan** and **skirt!** magazine

Shelf Life of a Trophy Wife touched my soul in more ways than one. Impossible to put down, it's an easy read that unveils the underlying issues that many women in today's society are scared to disclose. From child abuse to suicide to sipping Champagne with billionaires, it strikes every nerve in the best way. It's relatable, it's brilliant, it's an absolute must read."

Melissa Stanforth
Former casting agent, ***Real Housewives of Atlanta***

Lisa Kaye Rayner's memoir, *Shelf Life of a Trophy Wife* reveals a past full of secrets. Much like Julia Phillips's *You'll Never Eat Lunch in This Town Again* tongues will be waging from Atlanta to NYC upon its release. Lisa was born to please. Her Mother taught her to be polite, pleasing and to never leave the house without lipstick. Her life continues in this vein today but she is stronger, wiser, and driven by a sense of purpose to help others. As James Dickey is famously attributed for saying, "Southern women hold so many of its best kept secrets," and after all these years, Lisa is ready to talk!

Vikki Locke
former Atlanta Radio Legend

Why would she make this stuff up? That's a line that came to mind when I read this harrowing memoir by Lisa Rayner—my favorite (and third) ex-wife. While I might have preferred some of the tales she tells about me to be kept private, I guess that's not happening now! So I might as well admit, they are all true. The most sobering thing anyone can see is a reflection of themselves at their worst. Lisa, thank you for reminding me why I quit drinking, for humbling me in the aftermath, and for writing this book that will hopefully help others in need, or in support of finally revealing the truth.

Bill Tush
Former CNN Entertainment Correspondent,
TV Personality, Favorite (and third) Ex-Husband

What would happen if one woman told the truth about her life?
You're about to find out…"

Jack Watts,
Author of ***Hi, My Name is Jack*** and ***Recovering From Religious Abuse***

Shelf Life *of a* Trophy Wife

~ *a memoir* ~

LISA KAYE RAYNER

F **W**

Fitting Words

Nashville, Tennessee

Publishing services provided by Fitting Words LLC—Nashville, TN
To contact the publisher, visit: www.fittingwords.net

Print and eBook layout by Brian Kannard, bk@briankannard.com

Paperback ISBN: 979-8-9923952-0-4
Hardcover ISBN: 979-8-9923952-1-1

Printed in the United States of America

1 2 3 4 5 6 7 8 9 10

Author's Note

Shelf Life of a Trophy Wife is the blending of creative non-fiction and memoir—reflective nonfiction if you will. It is a tale of abuse, trauma, and grief, that blurs the lines between moments and memories in order to protect the author. Some characters were blended to spare comparisons, some names where changed, and some were left out altogether. As James Dickey is attributed for saying:

> Anyone who wants to get to know the South should get to know
> her women. They are tough, loving, frail and powerful. They hold
> so many of our best kept secrets.

Shelf Life of a Trophy Wife provides a glimpse into this Southerner's secret world… one that I hope you, the reader, will benefit from and hopefully my revelations will provide you some comfort in knowing that you are not alone. But be warned, it's not your mother's fairy tale.

Publisher's Note

I've engaged with many books over my long career as a bookseller, buyer, marketer, international publishing executive, and now publisher. But none has stopped and taken me back as much as *Shelf Life of a Trophy Wife*. Few things are as sad as when a person perceives they have a price but do not understand their true value. Some women will read this book in public - the rest in private. Either way, no man or woman will read Lisa's book without understanding the risks our sisters and daughters take when they open their hearts and lives to a potential partner.

Dan Wright
Publisher, Fitting Words LLC

For all my Graces

To my Mother Grace who gave me life and
my daughter Lydia Grace who saved it…

also

To Jennifer who left us broken and
To Kim who stayed to pick up the pieces…

Contents

Prologue 13

Chapter 1: Candle in the Wind 17

Chapter 2: Letter to My 4-Year-Old Self 27

Chapter 3: Stealing Kisses 34

Chapter 4: Cinderella Syndrome 39

Chapter 5: Edgewood Way 44

Chapter 6: Alone Again, Naturally 57

Chapter 7: Girl Sings the Blues 63

Chapter 8: Mean Girls 69

Chapter 9: Wild Horses 73

Chapter 10: Nowhere Road 83

Chapter 11: In the Midnight Hour 93

Chapter 12: Leopard is a Neutral 98

Chapter 13: How I Met Your Father 105

Chapter 14: I Don't Give a Damn, Frankly 113

Chapter 15: Lydia Grace 118

Chapter 16: Ring of Fire 124

Chapter 17: Sweet Caroline 128

Chapter 18: I Quit You Instead 135

Chapter 19: Dinner is Best Served Cold 141

Chapter 20: Curiouser and Curiouser 148

Chapter 21: Sweet Emotion 153

Chapter 22: Mother, May I?   158

Chapter 23: V is for Vindication   164

Chapter 24: Suicide is Painless   171

Chapter 25: Chapter and Verse   178

Chapter 26: Soul Sisters   182

Chapter 27: Three Can Keep a Secret…   188

Chapter 28: Hot August Night   198

Chapter 29: Make a Wish   204

Chapter 30: Like a Prayer   215

Chapter 31: Pearls Before Swine   222

Chapter 32: Friends in Low Places   226

Chapter 33: Nowhere to Go but Up   230

Chapter 34: After a While   236

Chapter 35: The Road Taken   240

Epilogue   249

Acknowledgements   251

Prologue

I am a writer. Or—I used to be. Lately it seems like I spend my days wallowing through some unknown, intangible state of uselessness.

Things that once felt important or meaningful have faded away into the abyss of memory. All that matters now is the fact that you are gone and the sad realization that there is nothing we can do to bring you back.

If only we had realized you were more a part of us than we knew. If only we had recognized that without you, we are not whole. If only we had taken the time to understand your struggle, we might not have to face a world without you in it.

I miss your laugh, your smile, your recklessness. I wish I could have fixed you, but I couldn't. I wish I had tried harder, but I didn't. I wish I could write down what I feel, but I am no longer a writer. I am no longer a little sister. I am no longer...

I wrote these lines after my sister, Jennifer, died by suicide in August 2005. The generic white loose leaf paper on which the words were written had long been misplaced—partly due to my grief, but mostly due to my carelessness, my unconscious inability to hold on to something so painful, and raw, and real.

Over the years, after many new moons and moving trucks, I finally accepted the fact that I had lost the loose leaf paper containing this haunting tribute to my big sister—until May 25, 2012, when I woke up from my own suicide attempt and found the note hiding behind the collected dust in the corner of my bedside table, gently resting next to my grandmother's well-worn Bible.

My attempt was not planned. It all happened so suddenly, so peacefully, that leaving a note was the last thing on my mind that stormy, humid May night in Georgia. But like a ghost of suicide's past, the next morning, there it was: My last note to Jennifer.

In that whimsical moment, a cloud of worry emerged through soft tears. Suddenly all I could think about was, "Did my oldest daughter, my unintentional savior, find this note?"

Did she think I was ending my life without saying goodbye to all of those I love and hold so dear? The truth is, I may never know, because the question was never asked, never answered.

The first lesson I learned as a budding Southern Belle was that we never address the uncomfortable things in life. We cover them up or simply sweep the bad under an impenetrable hand-knotted silk rug. Those dark moments in life are not the memories we prize, putting them on a shelf like well-collected treasures that are dusted off before company arrives. They are the ones we pretend didn't happen. We pack them away like out-of-date fashions, in hopes that one day we might be able to make them fit again. The problem with this way of dealing with our past, or not dealing with it, is that it is always there in the shadows, lurking like unfulfilled dreams that only come out at night when we are alone with our unconscious minds.

Like many of my contemporaries, we learned from our mothers to acquiesce to the men in our lives; to put our hopes and needs and dreams and futures on hold. I spent most of my prime career years championing my husbands instead of being a cheerleader for my own talents. In the end, this served no one, especially me. So after years of chasing someone else's dream, I finally "allowed" myself to put me first, and for the first time, I prioritized my goals and aspirations.

I tell you this with the hope that you might understand how hard it was to begin writing *Shelf Life of a Trophy Wife*. Not only did I have to try to dust off my past, but I also had to take my memories off the shelf, relive them, and outwardly acknowledge their existence. The incidents that were buried deep down in my soul, my darkest secrets, would now be laid out for all to see.

My hope is that you will find the courage to do the same.

Now, the secrets I kept in the shadows along with my flaws and fears are officially on display, and I am a writer once again.

LKR

Chapter 1
Candle in the Wind

I don't divorce well.

I dated well. I married well, on paper. But I did not divorce well.

I came to this conclusion while sitting in the reception area of a psychiatrist's office the Tuesday after Memorial Day, known to only me and a handful of friends as the first business day after the holiday weekend when I tried to end my life.

I was early; I am never on time, much less early. I always manage to find one more thing to cross off my list. If I have fifteen minutes before I am supposed to leave for an appointment, I take on a task that requires twenty-one minutes of my time. Thus begins the familiar dance of driving too fast, zipping through yellow lights, or taking the shortcuts necessary to arrive within the "fashionably late" timeframe. It was a trait I was known for, one that I owned. I never knew what it was like to be the first guest at an event, for I was always racing in at the last possible acceptable moment. And yet this day, I was early, awkwardly waiting to talk to a complete stranger and tell her what I could not answer myself—why I had tried, and failed, to die by suicide. My mind, not familiar with the concept of waiting, was racing so fast that I tried to concentrate on my surroundings in hope that the distraction might calm my nerves.

The office waiting room seemed to be frozen in time—walls of mauve and green speckle paint, popular in the early nineties, and a dark green carpet that was in desperate need of replacing. I was sitting in a flame-stitch patterned armchair that held the same hues as the walls that surrounded me. I hated the pattern; it belonged in a grandmother's dusty dining room, not a doctor's office. Its blurred lines and dated colors reminded me of myself, of what I had become, and of why I was here.

I looked at my fingertips to see if the blue tinge was still visible and thought, *All this fuss just because I tried to kill myself after a night of drinking margaritas with a guy ten years my junior?*

How do you explain a bad decision to a complete stranger when you can't even make sense of it yourself? It was such a peaceful decision, one not planned but rather induced by the amount of tequila I had consumed, followed by said guy's jealous fit of rage brought on by another man's attempt to get my phone number at our last bar-stop of the evening. That was when I realized that things were never going to change: I would always bring out the jealous nature in men; I would always bear the brunt of their insecurities, always be that object they desire but tell themselves they are unable to attain.

And then there was the rain.

Torrents poured down, so heavy that my Jaguar's aging windshield wipers struggled to keep up with the rainfall after I'd run to the security of my car to escape the very public outburst of my very angry date left standing at the bar. I couldn't decide which was pouring down faster, the rain or the tears that coursed over my blush-covered cheeks and puddled on my tanned legs below. To make matters worse, my old Vanden Plas suddenly went into "limp" mode; ironically, that's how I felt, too, as I made my way to my oldest daughter's college apartment in the tony northern suburbs of Atlanta—where I'd been staying for two years.

Pulling into the private garage under our place, I sat quietly, listening to the last notes of the Eagles song "Wasted Time" while the heavy metal door rumbled closed behind me. Suddenly, a calm came over me, and I made the decision to let the car run. Not before, but right in that moment. I pressed repeat on the stereo console and closed my eyes as I listened to the melodious music mix with the harsh reality of the running engine. I think I tried to sing along; I remember the bittersweet taste of my tears as I drifted off to the song.

The next thing I remember was the sound of the garage door opening, grinding slowly upward as if giving me time to get my bearings, awakening me from the ennui that had crept in uninvited. I recognized the sound of a car door opening, felt someone reach over my body, and then heard the quiet left by the engine being shut off. I struggled to open my eyes and looked up as my sweet Lydia cried, "Mom!"

"I thought you were going to your dad's," I said, simply. She helped me out of the car and closed the door softly on what would have been my tomb had she not found me. We walked between the trunk of the car and the open garage door, where the night air, once filled with rain, transformed into steam on the blacktop driveway. Lydia held my arm and guided me toward the open door to our apartment—the door I had run to two years earlier when I escaped from my last marriage.

Saying nothing, she led me up the stairs and into my room, removing the unchosen outfit I had left strewn across the bed a few hours before. My mind was foggy, and although I knew what was happening, I couldn't say a word. I began to lie down on the bed as she brought me water, which I drank without the familiar feeling of the liquid touching my mouth. The last thing I remember before drifting off to sleep was the gentleness of her holding my hand, checking my pulse.

I awoke the next morning in a panic and noticed that I was wearing the same black and white polka dot sundress I'd left the house in. Had I dreamed the events of the night before? My mind retraced my steps as I connected the dots and tried to figure out what I needed to do next. In a haze—one I still can't seem to shake—I reached for my cell phone to call my office and found it on the nightstand next to the bed. I noticed that the guy from last night had not bothered to check on me. *Nice*, I thought as I waited for my boss, CK, to pick up the phone at the luxury magazine headquarters where I worked in marketing. My voice was weak, and it cracked as I heard myself tell her that I had been in a car accident and would not be coming in that day—which, technically, wasn't a lie.

Lydia was supposed to be gone Thursday evening. She was going to her dad's for the holiday weekend, but she had changed her mind and, unbeknownst to me, was there when I arrived home. She would later tell me that she heard the noise of the garage opening, despite the pouring rain, then the sound of the garage door closing. Her bedroom was directly above the garage, but it took her mind a while to ascertain what was happening. Then, it registered: the noise she was hearing was the car engine running. She ran down (unknowingly) to save me, because it wasn't my time. I never really believed in that cliché, but now . . .

Now what? I thought to myself. I took a long, hot shower, hoping to wash off the strange numbness of the night, and tried not to look at myself in the mirror as I applied my makeup. Selecting a beige sundress, one that I had purchased for a date on Saturday, I slipped on some matching slingbacks and opened my bedroom door to face Lydia.

Instead, I found three of my best friends—Ellen, Kimberly, and Laura—sitting in different locations across the living room, almost as if they were ready to pounce in case I decided to run.

Then I saw Lydia emerge from her bedroom, standing quietly in the doorframe, afraid to join us. The look on her face reminded me of when she was a child and had been caught telling my secrets. I sat down on the closest chair and waited for them to begin the lecture.

Ellen was the first to speak: "Lydia called me this morning. She didn't tell me what happened at first; I had to drag it out of her, so don't be mad at her."

I started to cry as they all told me how special I was to them, how loved I was by them, how lucky they were to have me as a friend . . . as a mother. "But if you ever try to do this again, I'm going to kill you!" Laura said, somewhat jokingly. She then told me that she had called the office of a psychiatrist, a woman she had known before, and made me the first appointment she could get, which was the following Tuesday.

That is how, that Tuesday afternoon, I found myself sitting in a psychiatrist's office in an outdated Chippendale chair, waiting for my name to be called.

Lisa Kaye Rayner Kent Martin Tush . . . pick one, and I could tell you why each version of myself needed to see a doctor. Lisa Kaye needed a doctor to deal with experiencing her first French kiss at the age of 4. Lisa Rayner could have used intensive therapy to deal with being date-raped by a former boyfriend. Lisa Kent needed coping methods for marrying a compulsive liar. Lisa Martin needed someone to help her overcome the trauma of her pathologically jealous husband who, in true narcissistic style, kept her isolated from her friends and family. And Lisa Tush needed help moving on from the thought that her former-famous husband would stop the emotional abuse once she took him back after his stint in rehab for alcohol addiction.

I heard "Lisa Tush" and got up from my chair to follow the doctor down the hall to her office. "I'm Dr. H," she said by way of introduction. "May I call you Lisa?" I nodded yes, sat down, and waited for her to take her seat on the other side of the room. She looked at me with sad, knowing eyes; Laura had surely told her why I would be coming in today. Dr. H broke the silence and asked me where I wanted to begin.

"I know why she did it," I said, as I clutched my green leather Givenchy bag.

"You know why who did what?" she asked.

"Why Marilyn Monroe killed herself," I answered softly.

"Go on," Dr. H said as she began to write softly on her notepad.

"She was torn between being who they wanted her to be and being herself . . . between being a sex symbol and being a serious actor . . . between being used and being loved." I gently wiped the tears forming in the corners of my eyes so they wouldn't ruin my makeup or the emerald-green and white striped Ralph Lauren dress I'd chosen specifically for this occasion. It was a wise choice, if I do say so myself—a perfect ensemble for a shrink appointment and then my rescheduled date at a hotel bar for double dirty martinis.

The psychiatrist I'd been sent to, on the other hand, was wearing a nondescript chocolate brown dress and shoes. They matched her light brown hair and worn brown chair. So much brown. *She's pretty*, I thought, as I studied her deep brown eyes hidden behind large, red-rimmed glasses. I saw her beauty even though she hid it well. Her skin was flawless. But I could not make the connection between her dressed-down appearance and the lightness of her demeanor; she looked as much out of place in her office as I did.

"Do you want to be hospitalized?" Dr. H asked.

The matter-of-factness in her voice puzzled me almost as much as the question. Was there a choice? It's not like I was trying to decide whether I wanted fries with my order. Wasn't there some formula—an analytical tell, if you will—that a psychiatrist could use when they look at a new patient to ascertain whether they needed to be hospitalized?

"No," I answered, as matter-of-factly as the question was posed. "I want to follow in the tradition of my mother and pretend this never happened."

It was a Baptist thing. Or a Southern thing. Or a Southern Baptist thing . . . hell, I didn't know. What I did know was that if you press on and act as if something bad never happened, then it didn't count. You held your head up high and continued with life. It's easy once you become immune to the consequences and learn how to excel at the game of appearances. I learned how to sweep all the "bad" under the rug by watching my mother. And I learned from the best.

"What was your mother like?" she asked.

Taking a deep breath, I paused before I answered. My mother's soft Southern voice whispered in my ear, telling me not to speak of our family secrets—of Jennifer's mental illness, or my sexual tendencies, or Kim's feelings of not belonging. Don't speak of her dreams, of being placed on a pedestal where she was protected and no one could reach her. She often told us the only thing she ever wanted was security. Daddy gave her that.

But these were private things, of which no one ever spoke and of which I should never speak, especially to a total stranger.

"She was the most beautiful woman when she was young, though I didn't realize how gorgeous until I was much older. She is beautiful still," I managed to ignore the voice in my head and answered truthfully.

"So, she's still alive?" Dr. H asked.

"Oh, yes, very much so. As is Daddy," I answered. "She was a stewardess for Delta; that's where they met. Oh, and she went out with Elvis. *That's* how beautiful."

My mind took me back to when I was in second grade and she came into my classroom (she was the room mother). All the kids gathered around her like she was *magical*. They asked me if she was a movie star. I told them no, she was just my mother. She didn't work outside the home. She always said *we* were her job. When you become accustomed to being with such a gorgeous creature, you become immune to everything but *real* beauty. She was as smart, kind, and loving as she was beautiful. Perfect in our eyes, and in everyone else's too.

"I was in high school spending the night at a girlfriend's house when her mother said, very candidly, regarding my sisters and me, 'You three girls are pretty, but you will never be the beauty your mother is.' And her name, Grace. Such a perfect name for such a perfect woman." Suddenly, I was sad for my mother and what she, too, must have gone through. Her nightmares, for one, betrayed her carefully cultivated veneer of perfection. Every time I awoke to her crying in the black of night, it put another crack in her foundation, cracks only my sisters and I could see. Cracks that, over time, became caverns into which we all would fall.

But that day, to the therapist, I wasn't ready to reveal our secrets. Mother didn't believe in therapy, in airing your dirty laundry. In fact, there were very few things she did believe in. I thought of three right off the bat—The Father, The Son, and The Holy Ghost. And of course, family. She believed in the importance of family. Then there was the devil, love, and lipstick.

"She loved us and showed it daily," I said by rote. "'Every day is a gift,' Mother would say. During the week, she would wake us in the morning with a song, prepare breakfast for us, then drive us to school. When we would get home, we would go up the stairs to our rooms and find new clothes laying out on our beds—whole outfits with matching dresses, panties, socks, and shoes on display. She was always impeccably dressed for every occasion, and so were we. We had our school clothes, but then we would change into our play clothes when we got home. We had Sunday clothes for church and matching outfits for special occasions and holidays."

"It sounds as if you were her dolls," Dr. H commented.

"I guess we were. She wasn't close to her mother and would say she never felt her love. I think she was her father's favorite and maybe her mother—my grandmother—was jealous of her. Either way, she was determined to show us that she loved us. She was the youngest of five children; two boys followed by three girls. Her older sister, my Aunt Gail, was beautiful as well. I remember being in awe of Aunt Gail's beauty, but never of my mother's. They were both steel magnolias. I learned from the best how to hold my head up when bad things were said or done, and I'm talking brutally bad. It was expected that you just kept going on as if nothing happened, for appearance's sake."

"But this particular incident says the opposite to me," Dr. H said in a quiet, gentle voice. "What you did was a cry for help, which is why your friends sent you here."

"I wasn't crying for help," I explained. "I was letting go."

But the same thought kept creeping into my mind, *What will Mother think when she finds out I tried to kill myself?* She had yet to recover from my older sister Jennifer's death by suicide seven years earlier. And now, here I was, the near-perfect daughter who excelled at everything but marriage (and now suicide), trying to hide my sins like the good Southern Baptist girl I was brought up to be. Then, it hit me—Jennifer finally excelled at something I didn't. Death became her much more than life ever did.

"I was tired of being perfect, tired of worrying about what other people thought, and tired of apologizing for being smart, funny, or attractive. It was all so clear in my carbon monoxide-induced fog, when it dawned on me why Marilyn killed herself. She was tired of being herself in a world that didn't accept who she truly was," I told Dr. H. "And she didn't know who else to be. And I do not know who else to be."

"Interesting observation," Dr. H replied after my ramble. "Are you talking about Marilyn or yourself? It doesn't matter, does it? I'm going to give you twenty—" she looked at me again with her sad eyes, and, for the first time, I noticed how dark and mysterious they were. She paused and said, "No, forty milligrams of an antidepressant. I want you to go directly to the pharmacy and fill these. In addition to the Prozac, I'm giving you Trazadone. It should help you sleep. It will take a while for the meds to get in your system, but instead of next week, I think you should come in again on Friday. As part of my therapy, I assign a writing campaign where you write down your thoughts and explain your feelings. You can write a letter or note to anyone, as long as you are honest with yourself. And Lisa, be very honest. No one will see the letters but me. This assignment will help you delve deeper; not just to talk about what's on the surface, but to go beneath the tip of the iceberg and see what's underneath."

"I know what's underneath," I said. "And I don't want to go there."

"Let's see how you feel in a few days," Dr. H said as she handed me two pieces of paper. Instinctively, I noticed her nails. They were French manicured with red tips, so out of sorts alongside her frumpy brown dress and sensible shoes. "Oh, and Lisa, feel free to call me anytime. Here's my private number."

Taking the prescriptions and her card with a cell phone number written in blue ink, I made my way down the hallway to the checkout desk. I was numb, and vulnerable, and ready for a stiff drink. I would get that drink, and much more, that evening. Hopefully, once again, I would feel no pain. After thanking the person who took my $75 check written out to *psych.consult*, I left her office, tucked the scripts in my handbag, and went to meet the married man with whom I was about to consummate an affair.

Chapter 2
Letter to My 4-Year-Old Self

There's a strange calm that hovers over a shrink's office, as if all who enter are somehow now protected. The facades created to cover their hate, anger, paranoia, or hopelessness are exposed, and the realization that they are not alone quiets their inner demons. They feel safe, having accepted their flaws with the belief they are on a path to healing, learning how to "get better"—or at least learning how to cope. The veil has been lifted, and these patients feel a release, a willingness to share their secrets.

I was not one of them.

In fact, after my failed suicide attempt, I managed to go on about my life with little interruption. I went back to work, with a somewhat more sympathetic boss, at least for a little while. Her sheer joy in throwing me under the bus for things she'd done seemed to disappear, replaced by a desire to right her wrongs by telling my intern to "help her clean up this mess," referencing my cluttered office and paper-strewn desk.

My boss CK was a smart woman, but she wasn't "Southern smart." She had the looks, but her air of superiority, a product of her Northern upbringing, didn't fit in well with the well-heeled socialites who chaired and graced the patron parties and ballroom galas we so coveted to cover in the slick pages of our various publications. I could feel her resentment and jealousy of me because she knew that I was one of the chosen few who belonged to this circle of the A-listers. They were not just trophy wives, but doctors, lawyers, designers, heiresses, and businesswomen who owned their credentials and could keep up with their husbands' standing on their own accord.

Like Dante's *Inferno*, there were certain circles within which the Atlanta elite existed—each one nicer and more beautiful than the next. In fact, the smaller and more exclusive the circle, the nicer the people. I was lucky to be granted access, and I knew what it was like to be on the receiving end of their generosity after I divorced the man who'd gained entrance for us both. Unlike what most people would expect, my friends remained *my* friends. My status with them remained intact, for they were genuinely nice people. Rich, powerful, beautiful, nice people—and they were my friends.

After I divorced husband No. 3, he assured me they would drop me since I was no longer married to him. When at one of our "ladies who lunch" events, I mentioned this to the grande dame of our group, DS. She laughed so hard as she explained in her Southern drawl, "Darling, you will never not be included in our group. We *love* you; we just tolerated him because of you." This was something a Northern beauty wouldn't understand—that here in the South, it's not just what you look like on the outside that matters, it's also how you treat others and what is truly on the inside that counts.

I learned this a long time ago, when I was a little girl, by watching my mother. She was so kind and graceful, even to those who were not kind to her. Her star shone bright like a diamond, whether she was in a room full of people or alone in our home. I am deep in this thought when it was interrupted by a question.

"How do you feel today?" Dr. H asked as she peered at me from her lackluster desk, piled with papers and journals—a hoarder's cache of other people's defects. *Is she as fucked up as I am?* I wondered, as I thought back to Woodstock, New York, when I was introduced to a psychiatrist who came to one of our dinner parties when I lived there. Never had I met a woman spiraling so out of control. She was either high or drunk, or both. She needed a therapist more than I did . . . back then. I literally feared for her and asked my friend Rivka, who brought her to the dinner, if she thought her friend needed professional help. It was then I learned that she was a doctor, and she was in therapy.

While trying to find a response to her question, I spied a picture of a boy, about 7, in some kind of uniform, and an odd-shaped piece of pottery holding ink pens on Dr. H's crowded desk. *She's a mother to a young boy,* I thought; that explained a lot.

"I would like to revisit where we left off last time," she said. "Did you get a chance to write the letter?"

I handed her the note I had written on some of my old monogrammed stationery. It bore an M as the last initial, which made it about fourteen years out of date. Dr. H took the heavy cream-colored paper and adjusted the collar on her blue, white, and gold polyester diamond-patterned T.J.Maxx dress. (I knew her dress came from there because I had purchased the same one, in a different color, the day before.)

I had to return mine, though. I couldn't really justify new purchases when my AmEx bill was accruing interest on past ones. The truth was, I couldn't even buy food. I'd sold my $40,000 diamond engagement ring for $21,000, but that was months ago. That money had long been spent on rent, gas for my aging car, and champagne. I could cover my basic living expenses now with my full-time position in marketing, but any extra indulgences, like new clothes or accessories, were a hard *no.* Thank God I had enough designer clothes, shoes, and purses from my past lives to wear to all the special events I now was in charge of planning.

There was one dear friend in my close-knit social circle who knew this. I had not admitted anything about my current situation to anyone, especially to my family, since I did not want my parents or my surviving sibling to worry. But CCG guessed. She called me one afternoon, out of the blue, and asked if I was home; she was in the neighborhood and wanted to stop by my apartment. She brought me a goody bag, which contained some fabulous clothes, along with a Gucci scarf she "no longer wanted," some blush-colored tea roses, and, best of all, a $100 Kroger gift card. Bless her heart! That meant Lydia and I could actually buy groceries . . .

I wondered if my society and fashionista friends who invited me to charity luncheons or galas as their guest, or my coworkers with whom I planned magazine events, knew that those were the only times I ate? That my refrigerator, like that of a 20-year-old college student, contained only half-used condiments, for which there was no bread, meat, or cheese. There was champagne, of course—not the kind I had become accustomed to, but rather, the $4.99 bottle you find at Trader Joe's. *RSVP* was the name of the champagne, which I found very amusing. If we were lucky, there might be some leftovers from a dinner party, which I was no longer ashamed to take home. Still, there were always saltine crackers, packaged in twos and brought back from bars, restaurants, or fast-food establishments.

I thought to myself, *I'm as phony as the fake Louis Vuitton purse I'm carrying*, for I knew I would have to return the dress, along with the matching shoes and purse. Thankfully, some addictions were returnable.

What is it that addiction experts say about bad habits? They are a way of dealing with stress and boredom, and every habit is driven by a three-part loop—trigger, routine, and reward. But what I find most interesting is that the people who have the most self-control are the ones who are tempted the least, which rules me out on so many levels.

As Dr. H read the note I had written, I noticed the choices she made in her office decor. If the shared waiting room was decorated in the early nineties, her private office was a little less defined. Kirkland's must have had a sale on still-life paintings. The large, cerulean blue rug, which I was sure came from The Home Depot, had a Greek key border design that made it work in this space, but it was hidden by the furniture—mostly assorted faux leather brown chairs, a worn-out brown leather loveseat, and a dark blue denim couch. The 1990s called, and they want their denim couch back. Who used dusty blue as a paint color in any room other than a baby boy's nursery?

Then I remembered the picture on her desk. She is a mother, and I am sure she has better things to spend her money on than her office. I know I do.

I did think the lit candle was a nice choice. It smelled of the sea and calmed me while I waited for her to finish my letter: The one that I wrote to my 4-year-old self . . .

Dear Lisa Lu,

I wish I could save you from what you are going to experience in life, but I can't. I can't explain why you are going to have your first French kiss and be molested by Daddy's best friend at the age of 4. I can't explain how, instead of making you feel dirty, it is going to make you feel special. I can't explain that this pattern will continue until you try to close the door on your life.

It's not your fault. You will be told you "exude" sex; you will be hit on, grabbed, and fondled. You will be molested and told how beautiful you are, while the fathers of those you babysit drive you home, pull over on a side street, and stick their fingers inside you. You will develop well before any of the other girls, and those girls will hate you when their boyfriends pay you attention. You will be smarter than most in your class, but it won't matter. You will have your mother's beauty and classic hourglass figure, and your father's green eyes and sense of humor.

Adults will love you. And when you get old enough to consent, you will be drugged and raped when you say no. No one will respect you for your brains or take you seriously, so you will learn to play dumb and try to fit in. This will only make things worse. Married men will want you; single men will want you. But they will all be intimidated by your intelligence. They will be jealous of the way other men react to you. They will want to hide you away, like Hades did to Persephone, and keep you all to themselves.

You will resent the way you're treated and try to run away. And the men who can accept your sexuality will only want you for that . . . they will not want you as a wife. Only as a mistress. But you know in your heart, and in your mind, that you can be everything to them. It will not matter. You will end up alone. Get used to it. This pattern will never change, and you will never be able to change it.

Signed, Me

Dr. H placed the letter in her lap. "I think we have a lot to work on here."

"I decided to look under the iceberg," I replied.

There was a momentary silence; neither of us said a word. I hate silence. It's awkward, and it leaves me cold, lost, and anxious. I fought my way around thoughts of where to go from here. *Do I stand up and run out of her office* (as my flight instinct told me to)*? Or do I, for once, stay put in the moment and open up to her?* I decided on the latter and broke the silence with: "You know, it hasn't been *all* bad."

"What parts haven't been bad?" she asked.

"I had a glamorous life as a trophy wife, and I was very good at being one." I remembered the sudden thrill of being chased and courted with trips, gifts, flowers, cards, and love letters. And besides, it was what I had been groomed to be.

"It all happened so suddenly. One moment, I was a college-educated twenty-something working in PR, and the next, I was being sent flowers by older gentlemen. The flowers always came with invitations for weekend get-aways, complete with promises of shopping and champagne. I stayed in the private penthouse suite at Benny Binion's Horseshoe Casino in Vegas; I had tequila body shots in a private plane on the way to a yacht in Florida; I wore couture on the red carpet at The Oscars in L.A. and skied in Banff, Canada, at a Celebrity Sports Invitational event."

I paused and looked at Dr. H; she was expressionless. She stared at me as if she was listening intently, but she was not taking notes. Perhaps she ceased to be impressed long ago and now the circumstances of my visit proved her theory that it didn't matter what you had or who you had it with; if you were not happy, then you had nothing. Still, I continued.

"I've been kissed by the late comedian Jan Hooks in my kitchen in Woodstock, New York; I shared a boat outing with political columnists in Pensacola and a hot tub in Hawaii with the founder of Hawaiian Tropic. There was wine and conversation with an avant garde filmmaker and his publishing heiress muse at Shutters on the Beach in Santa Monica, and late-night laughter with many TV stars in New York. So yes, there were a lot of amazing opportunities that came with being a trophy wife."

"It pains me that you think of yourself as an object," she finally said. But her comment, and the look in her eyes, made me uncomfortable, so much so that I could feel myself revert to my inner child.

I never realized that I thought of myself as an object, but the way she looked at me . . . Suddenly, I understood what others must have seen all along. Although I had felt the safety and security of money, I also felt the loneliness and loss of being a sexual object. At the end of the night, I was still that small, scared little girl who looked up at the twinkling stars and wondered what life was all about, carrying the weight of my childhood insecurity and wondering—*Would I ever fit in?*

Chapter 3
Stealing Kisses

I was having a bad day. I knew this because I couldn't figure out what to wear for my appointment. It's not that I didn't have anything to wear. My wardrobe was extensive and just as varied as my moods; with this intensive therapy of going back to my childhood and reliving, for lack of a better word, "uncomfortable" events, I began to wonder if there wasn't more to my story than I was willing to acknowledge. I didn't know who to be anymore. I wanted to be that perfect child my mother always told me I was. I wanted to be the perfect wife, but that ship kept sailing without me. I wanted to be the perfect employee, but I was saddled with an impossible boss who seemed to be sabotaging my every move. Perhaps I was paranoid with the uncertainty that most likely came from surviving a tepid suicide attempt—an added burden, if you will.

If I were honest with myself, I could acknowledge the simple truth that I no longer wanted to hide my feelings, bite my lip, and say and do the right things. But, when I did express myself, those moments were explosions of emotions, and I would find myself asking, *Who is this person? Am I really crazy? Am I paranoid that the carefully painted picture of my perfect life is fading? Can you look behind the golden coral lipstick smile and see the damaged little girl begging to be saved?* Was it just me or did everyone feel this way at one time or another in their life?

Maybe Mother did know best—just keep silent and sweep the discomfort under the rug . . . and God forbid you look under it. Maybe that was the secret, after all: never look back or under or behind. I sighed and recrossed my legs as I waited in the Chippendale chair for my name to be called.

While I waited, I looked down to third guess the outfit I had chosen. I was wearing a Cynthia Steffe black pencil skirt and a sheer black blouse with white stitching that tied loosely at the neck. A black corset bra peeked ever so slightly through the sheer fabric, which made me feel as uncomfortable as I thought I looked. The skirt was a stiff cotton and came just below my knees when I was standing, but it managed to creep up past them when I was in a sitting position. The black patent pumps with five-inch stiletto heels I bought at Jimmy Choo in Phipps Plaza a few seasons back were snug on my feet. The temperature was in the eighties that day, but I didn't care. I had exchanged my summer sundresses for my femme fatale look, a decision I did not regret. At least, not until now.

Dr. H was wearing a red and white paisley patterned wrap dress with white shoes, never a good choice. I would just have to get over this fact as I followed her to her office.

"Are you going to a funeral?" she asked as we sat down.

"No," I replied.

I would never wear this outfit to a funeral, but I didn't tell her that. I hadn't a clue as to why I felt like bringing out a staple of my early fall wardrobe and wearing it on the last day of summer. I looked at her white open-toed shoes, and it dawned on me that she was wearing stockings. This was an even bigger faux pas than the "white after Labor Day" rule—said the broken girl dressed all in black in the middle of September.

"Stealing Kisses," she read out loud from the paper I handed over to her. "What's this?"

"It's a Faith Hill song . . . from her album *Fireflies,*" I said as she read the words to the song.

"And the significance of this is?" Her question lingered in the air between us as she raised her painted-on eyebrows to encourage me to finish her sentence.

"The significance is, I really don't know," I said, defeated. "I was listening to this song while I was taking inventory of my closet in anticipation of changing seasons, from summer to fall, when I found all my boots, including a pair of short white booties I thought were lost long ago. I had this 'flashback' of sorts. The only problem is, I can't remember."

"You don't remember the flashback?" She was confused.

"This is going to sound strange." I shook my head at the absurdity of the statement and continued. "But the boots brought back a memory, a story rather, of when I was a little girl living on Bowden Drive across from my parents' best friends—across from the man who first molested me. I guess it would have been 1965. I would have been 4. I had a pair of white go-go boots that apparently I wore *all* the time. I even slept in them. I do remember how much I loved those boots and wore them every day. But the story that IB and Mother always told, I do *not* remember at all."

"IB?" she asked.

"The wife of the man who gave me my first French kiss," I said. Actually, he was my father's best friend, who first stuck his tongue down my throat while I was sitting in his lap in the front seat of his Chevrolet, but what I said out loud about him sounded much better than what I remembered.

"They always told the story of the time I spent the night at their house, and after I fell asleep, IB, as we called her, came into the room and removed my white boots. When she did, out fell all these silver Hershey's Kisses. She laughed and surmised that I had stolen the kisses and hidden them in my boots. They always had candy sitting in a colored glass dish in their house, which was such a Southern thing to do. So it was feasible that I could have taken the candy and hidden it in my boots."

"But you don't believe you stole the kisses?" She wrote something in her notebook.

"No, I don't. I can't for the life of me remember stealing the candy or putting the silver kisses in my boots. We were taught better. We didn't lie, or cheat, or steal. Maybe I was too young to remember?"

"Or there's another possibility," she stated matter of factly, a slight gleam in her eye.

"Yes, that's what I was wondering too. Maybe I don't remember putting the kisses in my boots because I didn't."

"Who do you think . . ." She didn't finish the question.

"You know who . . . *he* did. Maybe he told me he would bring me a surprise if I would go to sleep? Maybe he snuck into the room where I slept and did things to me? Maybe he's the one who put the candy in my boots, and I was the one accused of stealing kisses?" *I honestly have no memory either way*, I thought as I asked the last question.

"The mind is a remarkable organ." She started her doctor-speak, but I didn't listen. I knew the drill. The scientific data that documented the facts that our memories do not really take hold until we are around 4. I knew that painful memories at such a young age could be repressed, buried, and never see the light of day unless something was triggered, dug up, and brought out into the open. *Didn't I suffer enough damage with the abuse I could recall?*

All I'd done was find an old moving box in the back of my closet labeled "Early Fall." How could I have known that rifling through its contents would carry me back to a long-forgotten memory? Memories of fallen leaves, golden yellow, amber, and rust; of lying on the ground and watching them take flight. Of Daddy raking the newly scattered leaves in big piles and of three girls jumping in the middle like a Little Golden Book story of a picture-perfect day. These are the childhood memories I wished to remember.

I pondered this as I looked down at my choice of outfits for today, and I thought, maybe I *would* have worn this ensemble to a funeral. To his funeral.

Chapter 4
Cinderella Syndrome

Leaving early from my "ladies who lunch" dates was always difficult, but having to leave for an appointment with my psychiatrist was doubly hard. *Do I tell my innermost secrets to a professional and not share them with my closest friends? My friends who have been with me through a couple of husbands and a few bad choices in "boys who were friends"?* It was hard to keep up appearances of "normal," whatever that was. Who was it that said "normal is a setting on a dryer"?

It was DS's birthday luncheon at the café at Neiman's. Everyone was sad to see me go, but none more than my precious D, my favorite redhead, next to Ellen. But D knew why I had to go (she always knew), and her gracious excusal of my departure made leaving so much easier than if she had asked me to stay. For this is what we ladies who lunch do best: we linger.

Some in attendance were probably suspicious of my excuse to leave, not because it wasn't believable, but because of what I was wearing—a crisp white collared shirt and black-and-white houndstooth pencil skirt with Jimmy Choo boots. This is not what one wears to get a pedicure, but I made my way out of the luncheon with ease, thanks to D's suggestion that I get going lest I be late for my spa appointment.

I arrived with time to spare and noticed that, after almost five months of therapy, sometimes twice a week for one hour each session, Dr. H had made certain she has a sea-scented candle lit for me. Her office smelled of the beach, which happens to be my place, my solace.

"I've decided that the only hell we have to face is the one we choose to live here on earth," I began immediately upon sitting down on the familiar couch.

"If I had to choose a heaven, it would definitely have an ocean with white-capped waves, soft white sand, bright yellow sun, and, of course, the saltiness of the sea. I would spend hours with my feet in the emerald-green waters, letting the waves rush over me. Just like we did when we were little, and Mother and Daddy took us to the beach in Florida for a week in June each year when school was out for the summer.

"We would go to bed early on that last Friday of school in preparation of getting up at four a.m. I remember closing my eyes after prayers, and the excitement of the trip was almost more than I could stand. I was always the last to fall asleep, and I would try to find a happy place. Sometimes Daddy would come in and rub my feet to try and help me relax. He understood what it was like to have trouble sleeping. Mother, Jennifer, and Kim could put their heads on their pillows and be asleep in an instant. Not me. I had a hard time getting my mind to shut down.

"Anyway, we would be rustled out of bed while the Georgia moon was still up, carried to the car with our pillows, and the next thing we knew, it would be nine a.m. and we would be stopping for breakfast." I took a sip of the sparkling water I had been bringing to my appointments. It's LaCroix, grapefruit-flavored, my favorite. I usually drink half the can before I arrive, then fill it back up with white wine, usually Sauvignon Blanc, and sip on my wine spritzer during my session. No one knows this; it's my little secret—my way of getting through telling the truths behind why I am here.

"I always ordered country ham and hash browns. That's my favorite breakfast.

"I look back at those trips and often wonder what Mother and Daddy would talk about for their five hours of undistracted driving three little girls to the beach. They never argued in front of us.

"Daddy was and *is* very funny; I think that's why a good sense of humor is so important to me in a man. I need someone who can make me laugh.

"We would sleep the entire way from Georgia, to whatever Florida beach town they had chosen for us to visit, unless Daddy stopped suddenly. We had a 1958 coral and white Edsel. I was usually in the rear window bay, Jennifer in the seat, and Kim on the floor. So if Daddy stopped, we would end up on the floorboard on top of Kim.

"One night stands out in my memory; it was in June 1968. I know this because we woke up when my parents turned up the radio. Robert Kennedy had been shot, and they were listening to the news. That's the second tragic death I have any memory of. The first one was the death of my Uncle Bob in Athens. For years, I thought it was President Kennedy who had been shot, then later I realized it was the news of his brother's assassination I'd been listening to."

"You would have been . . . how old?"

"I had just turned 7," I told her. "I think I realized the magnitude of the event by how my parents reacted to the news. They were so sad and whispered about the tragedy, not knowing that I was awake and listening to their conversation.

"I can't figure out if I have deep memories of all our trips to the beach because they were so magical; or if they are such deep, magical memories because I can look at the photos from that time and am transported back. I see us on the beach making sandcastles, playing by the pool. I remember Jennifer and me jumping the waves, holding onto Daddy's hands as his strength pulled us up in the air so the waves did not splash in our eyes.

"I guess Kim was too little to be with us in the water. She was always with Mother. But Jennifer and I would spend the day in the sand and the sea, and I remember the taste of the salt on my lips. Perhaps that's why I enjoy a salted rim on my margaritas." I smiled. She didn't.

"Anyway, I think I have such a strong attachment and love of the beach because those were some of my fondest childhood memories."

"It stands to reason," Dr. H said. "You felt safe there."

"I never thought of it in terms of feeling safe," I said. "But yes, I guess that's why the beach is so calming to me. I do feel safe and young and unburdened. Even today when I go to the beach, I am that little girl, playing in the sand with her sister by her side. I still feel her presence with each grain of sand that filters between my toes. Maybe that's why I dig them so deeply in, as if to find that place that's just ours.

"There is one time, though . . . Let's say, an *incident* . . . during a trip to the beach that still haunts me."

"Still? To this day?" she asked.

"Yes, my mind will take me back to this one moment. I don't know how old I was, probably 4, maybe even before I was molested. I was at the pool with adult supervision: Mother or one of her friends. I was heading back to the beach house and was walking along the flat stone path when this man—I guess he was a man, but I really don't know how old he was—anyway, I noticed this huge bug, I think it was a palmetto bug. I stopped in my tracks looking at this very large, very scary bug when this guy picked it up and started chasing me with it. I ran as fast as my little legs could go, running back to the beach house, yelling out for Daddy. When I got to the door, Daddy came running out and saw this man chasing me.

"I ran inside and slammed the door. I never found out what happened after that. I'm certain Daddy must have said something to the guy. I only remember being chased by this man with a bug, running as fast as my little legs could take me, and yelling out for my father to help me."

"Cinderella syndrome," she said. "It's the classic case."

"That's been my issue all along," I said, thinking it was the perfect diagnosis given my obsession with shoes and being saved.

"And your idea of hell?" she inquired.

"You've listened to me," I replied. "Don't you think I'm living it?"

Chapter 5
Edgewood Way

Being medicated was not what I thought it would be. It had been six months since I first sought help after my suicide attempt, and I wasn't feeling the effects of the meds like I thought I should. Dr. H explained to me that it would take a few weeks for the Prozac to get into my system, but I was beginning to wonder if this "miracle mood enhancer" had any real power over me at all. Could it be that the champagne I was chasing my pills with caused the drug not to be as effective? Or maybe my numbness stemmed from a lifetime of conforming to religious rules and maintaining my mother's persona of perfection? But I didn't want to tell Dr. H this; I didn't want her to tell me to stop drinking. So I kept this little bit of information to myself. Again, I was hiding painful truths so that the good Southern Baptist woman that I was would not be set up for ridicule.

I found myself anxious; wait, wasn't this drug supposed to quell that emotion? My heart was racing, and I had the distinct feeling of wanting to crawl out of my skin. I looked down and reevaluated my outfit choice for the day—a new, long black T-shirt dress with the words *More Issues Than Vogue* emblazoned in white block letters across my chest. I found the dress on sale at a high-end retailer shortly after my first session and my disastrous date afterwards with the married man who pressured me into meeting him for "just a drink." I still can't believe I fell for that. Again. It's never just a drink. They will tell you that they just find you "interesting" and want to get to know you better, that perhaps you could do some PR work for their company—but there was always something more that they wanted. You agree to meet for a drink, or for lunch, or coffee, and it turns into a conversation about how sexy you are; how they can't stop thinking about you; oh, and by the way, do you want to spend Christmas in Vegas? Who leaves their husband unsupervised over any major religious holiday?

"Sorry about that," Dr. H said as she walked into her office, explaining why she left me alone for a few minutes. "What's this?" She took the stack of papers from my hands and, out of sync from our previous sessions, sat down on the couch across from me.

"Did I tell you I'm taking a screenwriting class at Emory?" I answered a question with a question, which was so out of character for me. I was the obedient child, the good girl who always played by the rules—not this warped ball of raw nerves sitting in a psychiatrist's office doped up on Prozac and champagne.

"It's a screenplay based on a precious childhood memory. I decided to combine my 'homework,'" I said, actually making air quotes with my Lincoln Park After Dark manicured nails that I really couldn't afford anymore. It was my "go-to" fall color. "You asked me to write about my feelings, and my Screenwriting 101 professor asked me to write about a precious childhood memory, so I combined the two assignments."

Sitting in silence, on the blue denim couch with too many throw pillows, I took in the scent of the beach candle while she put on her red readers and concentrated on what I had written.

Closing my eyes, I thought about what she was reading, and I was instantly transported back to that night at the end of summer in 1969 on Edgewood Way.

I was back in the house I grew up in, where all my formative memories and experiences, good and bad, were stored. I smelled the intoxicating scent of my mother's perfume and saw the turquoise-colored sofa with the silver threads that were woven into the psyche of my childhood as much as they were woven into the fabric itself. Edgewood Way; the house where my journey with my sisters began; the house that was given to Jennifer in hopes of "fixing" what made her different. The house where she would choose to end her life.

But the story I had written began much earlier, before we realized just how brilliantly wicked Jennifer was or were able to admit that her childhood actions were most likely caused by mental illness.

I had just turned 8 years old and was petite for my age, with summer blonde hair and sun-kissed olive skin. It was the third Friday of September. I had stopped to pick a dandelion to take to my mother, but the weed's petals drifted away as I skipped across the green grass and up the stairs to our kitchen door. I walked in, stem in hand, and waited for my mother's attention as I listened to her talk on the phone.

She was standing at the counter, chopping vegetables and throwing them into a large wooden bowl already full of shredded iceberg lettuce. She spoke with the receiver cradled on her shoulder, while the long, dirty-beige spiral cord stretched across our Harvest Gold kitchen, swinging and dipping in sync with the movements of her body.

"No, Bunny," Mother said. "They are either babysitting for everyone else, or they won't come back because of Jennifer. Apparently, word has gotten around that she tied up our last babysitter during a game of war. I know! It was only for a little while. Anyway, if you can think of anyone, please let me know. I really don't want to miss the block party again. I'm prepping my salad just in case. I'll send Lisa over for the salad tongs."

Mother walked to the wall to hang up the phone and looked at me. I knew what she was going to ask, so I handed her the stem and said, "I'll go get the salad tongs from Mrs. Ambers, Mother." Then I skipped back outside and down the stairs and crossed up the grassy hill that led to our neighbor's house.

Our house was the biggest in the modest, middle-class neighborhood, slightly south of Atlanta; a split-level in that early '70s *Brady Bunch* style, except it was red brick with white columns and sat on a corner lot. The Amberses' house was a white brick ranch whose carport had been turned into a keeping room off the kitchen. This was the door at which I presented myself and rang the bell. I looked through the screened door and saw Mrs. Ambers on the phone. I watched as she handed the salad tongs to her 16-year-old son, Chipper. He was dressed in white tennis clothes and balancing a yellow tennis ball on his racket when he answered the door. I felt a bit strange, standing there in my white-eyelet sundress and pink plastic Barbie heels.

I smiled at him, revealing a couple of missing teeth.

"Mother sent me to borrow the salad tongs," I said.

He held the tongs up in the air and asked me, "What's the secret word?" as if I were a dog begging for a treat.

"Please?" I responded, holding out my hand for the tongs. He dropped them on the floor and walked away, still balancing his tennis racket in hand. When he got back to the kitchen, I heard him ask his mother, "Who needs a babysitter?"

I picked up the tongs and headed back the short distance to our house, not bothering to pick another flower along the way. Instead, something else caught my eye. I stopped and marveled at a large black fuzzy caterpillar making its way up the dogwood tree in our yard.

Curiosity got the best of me, so I was startled when Jennifer came up behind me and yelled, "What'cha doin', princess Barbie!?" Jennifer, who was eighteen months older than I, was all tomboy—her long, brown hair was in pigtails, and she was wearing cutoff jeans, a faded black T-shirt, and used-to-be-white Keds. We shared the same parents, green eyes, and a bedroom, but absolutely nothing else.

"I'm watching this fuzzy caterpillar climb up our tree," I answered.

"*Duh*," she said. "I can see that. I can tell you something about that bug that you probably don't know."

"It's not a bug. It's a very large fuzzy black caterpillar," I replied.

"Technically, it's a giant leopard-moth caterpillar, also known as a tiger-eyed moth." She leaned in closer and pointed to the caterpillar. "See the black hairy spikes, or the fuzzy parts, and the red bands around here?"

I leaned in for a closer look and listened as she told me that this creature that looked like a black wooly bear will turn into a white moth with black spots, like a leopard's, on its wings.

"How do you know so much about this caterpillar?" I asked, leaning in even closer.

"We just learned about this in school," Jennifer said as she motioned for me to take a closer look, which I did. Then, without a word, Jennifer raised her hand to my back and pushed me into the tree. When I pulled away, the fuzzy caterpillar had been smashed onto my white-eyelet dress, staining it with blood, guts, and black fuzz. Still holding on to the tongs, I found myself catching my breath; I could feel the tears well up in my eyes, while my big sister ran away, laughing.

Mother, who heard my screams of terror, came running out the door to see what Jennifer had done to me. She held me in her arms and told me she could probably get out the stains from the caterpillar, which was now crushed into the crevices of fabric. She wiped my tears and took me inside to change. "We'll tell your Daddy all about this when he gets home," she whispered, as she ran a bath for me to wash all the hurt away. "It was time to put away that dress anyway."

By the time I got downstairs, Daddy, still in his golf attire, was sitting at the kitchen island sipping sweet tea, while Jennifer and Kim sat at the table blowing on their Swanson chicken pot pies Mother had made for dinner. Mother, dressed in black capris, a classic white button-up blouse, and kitten heels, placed salad on the plates and returned to the counter to get my dinner.

As she motioned for me to sit, she looked at Jennifer and asked, "Are you going to tell your father what you did to your sister today, or shall I?"

Jennifer looked back and forth between me and Kim before she asked, "Are you talking to me?"

"Don't add *smart aleck* to your list of sins, Jennifer Lynn. You know good and well I'm speaking to you."

"What happened now?" Daddy asked, not knowing what was coming next or how serious the incident would be. This was Jennifer, after all.

"Jennifer slammed Lisa into the dogwood tree in the front yard," she answered.

"I see," was all he said.

"No, you don't," Mother replied. "Lisa was watching a caterpillar climb the tree, and Jennifer came up behind her and knocked her into the poor thing. Smashed the creature directly in the middle of her outfit your mother sent her for her birthday. I've been soaking it all day, and I don't know if I can get the stain out."

"And what do you want me to do?" my father asked, picking a piece of cucumber from the salad on Kim's plate.

"I've been dealing with Lisa all afternoon, trying to console her. I told Jennifer you would deal with her as soon as you got home, so that's what I want you to do." Mother said, emphatically.

"I see," my father replied, before whispering under his breath, "Says the blind man." Then, "and that would be now?"

I smiled as I blew on my chicken pot pie, still too hot to eat. Jennifer rolled her eyes while Kim picked all the peas and carrots out of her dish and placed them on top of her salad to make up for all the cucumbers Daddy had stolen. Mother took off her apron, grabbed Kim, and held her hand out to me.

"Yes, that would be now," Mother answered. "I'm taking the girls up for their bath while you and Jennifer sort this thing out."

Mother left the kitchen with us in tow, while Daddy got a beer from the refrigerator and looked at Jennifer as she shrugged her shoulders.

He simply said, "Don't do that again to your sister."

"Yes, sir," she replied, as she headed up the stairs for her bath.

I was in my room, having already taken a bath that day, while I listened and tried to figure out who Daddy was talking to in the foyer. I peeked over the open balcony and saw Daddy in a leisure suit with a colorful, silk-printed shirt, talking to Chipper Ambers.

"Well, come on in and sit . . . after all these years, I still don't know what takes her so long." Daddy opened the faux Oriental bar cabinet and fixed a drink of bourbon and Coke. Chipper sat on the other side of the room, uncomfortable on the fancy turquoise sofa with silver threads. "She's beautiful without all that extra stuff she puts on her face. But you can't say anything; otherwise, we'll be here another hour while she adjusts," he laughed and took a sip of his cocktail.

Mother finally entered the room wearing a short "Pucci-esque" print dress and high-heeled gold shoes. She was always in heels. The scent of Chanel N°5 filled the room. She stood between the bar and the loveseat.

"I could hear you all the way up the stairs," she reminded him as she walked in the formal living room. "Chipper, thanks so much for watching the girls. Kim is already asleep, Jennifer is being punished in her room, and Lisa is getting into her PJs. They've all been fed, so all you have to do is make sure they go to bed by nine."

Daddy picked up a glass of a mint green concoction and handed it to Mother. Smiling her thank you, she took the grasshopper cocktail and continued her instructions. "OK, Kim, is already asleep. Lisa can watch her shows on TV, but Jennifer is not allowed. And absolutely *no one* is allowed in this room."

"I guess that includes me!" Chipper said, as he started to get up and clumsily knocked down a porcelain vase from the wooden sconce above his head. He caught it before it fell to the ground.

Mother took the cream and gold antique vase from his hands and replaced it on the sconce before saying, "Well, yes, that includes you."

"Don't worry, Chipper, I'm only allowed on this side of the room," Daddy told him with a laugh.

I was dressed in my favorite *I Dream of Jeannie* lavender PJ set, and Jennifer wore her go-to cotton T-shirt and short PJ bottoms as we frolicked down the stairs and kissed our mother goodbye. She was so beautiful. Her elegant stance and quiet ways made her even more so. She told us to be good for Chipper, not to forget to brush our teeth if we have a snack, and that bedtime was in two hours.

"If you wait any longer, *you* can put them to bed yourself, honey," Daddy said as he looked at his watch.

"Very funny, dear. Okay, we won't be late. And Chipper, you know we'll be with your parents just up the street if you need us."

Daddy paused under the light on the front porch and asked, "You think Chipper's okay to sit with the girls?"

"Now who's being sensitive? Bunny says he watches Cindy all the time. Besides, what are we going to do now? We're already late, and we have the salad!"

"I guess you're right, but I forgot the tongs." He grinned the smile that always got him out of trouble.

"Oh, Richard! Well, we can't go back in . . . it will take us another fifteen minutes to say goodbye."

Dr. H finally looked up from the pages I wrote for my dual assignment. "I think I know where this is going," she said, somberly.

"Where are you in the story?"

"Your parents have just left you and your sisters in the hands of your neighbor's 16-year-old son."

"Oh, so you haven't gotten to the good part yet?" I asked with a smile.

"I'm not sure I want to read about the 'good' part," she answered.

"Well, I can assure you that whatever you have in your mind as to what happened next, you will *never* guess right."

"I didn't mean to take up all of our time reading," she admitted. "I wasn't prepared for you to bring such a long story."

"If you're worried about me, don't be. I'm just anxiously awaiting your reaction when you read what happened that night . . . and if you think this isn't one of the reasons why I am here, you are wrong. You see, I have never told this story to anyone, much less put it in writing, so this has been very cathartic for me."

"That's why I assign this form of therapy," she said with a comforting smile as she picked up the pages and fell back into my story.

Jennifer and I were in the den, lying on the rug in front of the wood-paneled TV set watching *The Brady Bunch*. Chipper was sitting on the early-American sofa, which was a horrible old-gold color. It was a hand-me-down from my paternal grandparents that seemed as dated and stiff as they were. He was looking at his watch. He began to argue with us over bedtime, and then he proposed a deal. He would let us stay up longer if we would dance for him.

"No way," Jennifer crossed her hands in defiance.

"I'll do it," I said.

"No, you won't!" Jennifer piped up.

"I love to dance! I dance all the time. I was a sunflower in the ballet last year."

"You fell off the stage during the performance," she reminded me. "Besides, that was different. I'm not going to let her do it."

Jennifer was looking at Chipper, and I wasn't quite sure who would win this battle. Jennifer climbed the stairs, but she didn't go to her room. Instead, she hid behind the desk in the loft above the TV room and watched as Chipper turned the volume down on the television and put a record on. Doris Day's "Hooray for Hollywood" blared through the speakers.

"Now, this dance is called a striptease," he grinned.

"I don't know that dance," I said.

"Do you really want to know how to do it? 'Cause to do it right, you have to dance and take off your PJs at the same time." Chipper was smiling.

"Why would I do that?" I asked.

"'Cause that's how you do a striptease."

Chipper came over to me and started to take down the cap sleeve of my *I Dream of Jeannie* pajama top. Obediently, I took the other one down. Then he stepped back and watched as I started to remove it. He told me to take it off and throw it to him, which I thought was silly, but I did it anyway.

I threw the little lavender top at him and felt sick to my stomach as I covered my small, eight-year-old breasts with my hands. Then he motioned for me to remove my harem pants. I began to dance like Chipper showed me and slowly slid my pants down around my ankles before kicking them off in his direction. I was standing in the middle of the den, wearing only my Saturday panties with my arms still wrapped around my bare, flat chest.

"Now dance for me," he demanded.

"No! This isn't fun anymore. I changed my mind," I said, as I ran up the stairs, leaving Chipper on the sofa holding my pajamas.

Jennifer pretended to be asleep while I opened the dresser drawer and took out a yellow nightgown. Climbing into my matching twin bed, I tried to go to sleep, but my mind was racing.

"Why did you do it?" Jennifer whispered.

"I don't know. I wanted to, I guess."

"No, you didn't," she said. "You just didn't know how to say *no*. It was wrong. You know that, right?"

"Yes, I know." I took a deep breath and turned to face her, tears streaming down my face.

"Well, I'm not going to let him get away with it," Jennifer said defiantly.

"You can't tell mom. I don't want to get in trouble."

"I'm not talking about telling anyone," she answered. "I have a plan."

"Your plans always get us in trouble," I replied with worry.

"Not this one. Trust me."

"What are we going to do?" I sat up in bed and rubbed my eyes.

"We're going to wait until he falls asleep," she answered.

"How do you know he'll go to sleep?"

"They always do," she said. "I know. I'm always the last one up."

Jennifer was right. We looked down from our perch and saw that Chipper was passed out on the sofa in the living room, with an empty bottle of Jack Daniels and a sterling silver mint julep cup on the floor by his side. Jennifer peered over the banister and threw one of my little plastic Barbie purses down to the ground. It landed with a quiet clink in the mint julep cup.

"Shoot, I couldn't have done that if I was trying," she rumpled her face. "Don't you have anything that will make more noise?"

I handed her a large, oval "cocktail" ring that Mother bought me from the novelty store. Jennifer took the big metal ring and threw it down below. I watched with wonder as the large fake stone swirled in the air like an emerald prism, raining facets of green as it caught the light of the hallway chandelier. This time, the tossed object hit the cup and made a louder sound. Chipper still didn't move. Jennifer looked at me and smiled her crooked smile.

"OK. Let's move," she said, as she grabbed her Army-green duffel bag. Of course, I was wearing my Barbie heels that made a *clip-clop* noise as we descended the hardwood steps.

"Take those off, stupid!"

"Sorry," I whispered, as I removed the pink plastic heels.

We reached the living room and huddled on the floor by the bar. Jennifer opened up her duffel bag and searched for scissors and string. I watched her with a confused look on my face.

She whispered for me to go to the kitchen and get the salad tongs from the counter.

I tiptoed to the kitchen and knocked into the kitchen chair, turning around as if to say, *I'm sorry*. Jennifer was not looking at me; she was cutting the string and moving toward the couch. When I came back into the room with the tongs, she had already unbuttoned Chipper's shorts and was unzipping them. I dared not ask; the perplexed look on my face said it all—*What am I witnessing?*

"Tongs." Jennifer was barely speaking loud enough for me to hear as she extended her hand toward me, like a doctor in an operating room.

I handed her the tongs and watched in horror as she took them and inserted them into the opening of Chipper's white boxer shorts. Fishing around, she pulled out (what I now know was) his penis. She gave the tongs back and instructed me to hold them steady. I did exactly as she said, and watched, wide-eyed, as the organ grew before me.

Jennifer took the string and tied one end around Chipper's erect penis, as I held tight to the tongs, squeezing them together.

"Not so tight," she whispered.

"Sorry," I mouthed back to her in response.

Then Jennifer took the other end of the string and tied it around the wooden bracket holding one of Mother's prized antique vases. I gave her a look that said, *We're going to get in trouble*.

She took the tongs from me and stuffed them under the sofa. Then she grabbed her bag and held my hand, as we made our way back up the stairs.

When we reached the landing, we turned around to look at what we had done. I can still see the image in my mind: Chipper Ambers lying on the now-tainted turquoise sofa, with its silver threads shining in the light of the chandelier. His shorts open and his enlarged penis floating in mid-air, hoisted by a string that was tied to the bracket on the wall above the sofa that held Mother's prized antique vase.

Jennifer smiled down at the vision, admiring her handiwork. I slipped back on my Barbie shoes before we both ran to our room and jumped back into our beds. We never saw—or heard from—Chipper again.

Dr. H finished reading the pages, took off her glasses, and placed the script in her lap. I waited for her to comment. "So, this really happened?"

"Everything I tell you, it happened. Whether it's spoken in this office or written down on paper, per your instructions," I said.

"It's very hard to believe," she confessed. "What did your parents say when they returned home?"

"That's the best part," I responded. "There was never anything spoken. Still, to this day, I don't know if my parents came home and found him in the living room with his penis tied to the sconce on the wall. It was never brought up; we were never questioned; and Jennifer and I never spoke about the incident again."

"Well, I would like to explore your relationship with your sister, Jennifer. It seems she had quite an impact on you."

"She had an impact on us all," I said.

Looking back, I always thought Jennifer was the strongest of us, but maybe I was wrong. She was tough and powerful; I was the frail one. Yet she gave up on life, on us.

And then I thought about what life was like on Edgewood Way in small-town Jonesboro, Georgia, and I realized I was finally ready to visit certain parts of my past, long hidden in the chamber of my mind labeled "childhood" that contained secrets of Jennifer's mental illness, how it encompassed our world, and how we all spent our lives trying to save hers.

Chapter 6
Alone Again, Naturally

"I didn't realize how sheltered I was as a child until I went to junior high school," I begin. I was wearing dark skinny jeans and black suede Manolo Blahnik stilettos, a black long-sleeved T-shirt that read *I Don't Love You Anymore,* with Chanel pearls and lots of bangles. I carried a pony-skin clutch under my arm like a trophy. Once again, I was dressed for the occasion.

"Looking back on those times, there really should be a better transition from elementary school with nap time and recess to junior high with hormonally mean girls and testosterone-fueled boys."

"Sounds as if you had a difficult time transitioning, and that surprises me."

"Why?" I was curious.

"Because you appear to be someone who has made every transition with ease. For you to be caught up in this move from elementary to middle school seems like it would be insignificant."

"Not when you factor in the 'mean girls' element. I was not prepared to encounter a group of girls who totally did not like me nor want me in their group. It was something very foreign to me, and it was a defining moment in my life that changed the way I looked at people."

She recognized my voice cadence, the rhythm I speak in when I am concentrating on my past, and per her usual, she let me continue without interruption.

"School came easy to me. I was always one of the 'smart' kids in the class. The straight-A student whom teachers loved. I was a nice girl and had many friends. Everything came easy to me, and I thought that was how life was, until seventh grade at Mitchell Junior High.

"Over the summer I tried out for cheerleading for the school's seventh- and eighth-grade team. I was one of the two to make the team, and I was overjoyed and proud to be one of the two seventh graders to be chosen.

"I still remember how it felt after I received my MJH Cheer T-shirt. The coaches had all the girls sit down on the gymnasium floor and wait while they made their decision. Then they had the graduating cheerleaders run around us with the cheerleading shirts, and you knew you were chosen when they stopped in front of you and presented you with the shirt. I was so excited. My parents were waiting outside in the car—we were heading to a weekend lake trip with friends—and when I came running out with my big smile and wearing the cheerleading shirt they got out of the car and gave me a big hug. Then off we went. I can still feel the excitement as I laid in the back of the car listening to 'I can't stop this feeling.' You know, the song 'Hooked on a Feeling,' the version by Blue Swede that starts with a chorus of 'Ooga-Chaka.' Whatever that means.

"Anyway, where was I? Oh yes. Unfortunately, the other five members of the squad were not too happy I was on their team. It seems that the girls had all gone to the same elementary school and had known each other for a long time. One of their best friends also tried out for the squad and they had all hoped she would be the one chosen, but I beat her out. I ended up being an outcast on the team."

"For someone like you, who has always been able to breeze into your life's situations, I am sure that was difficult." *She understands*, I think to myself.

"*Difficult* is not the word I would use," I said sadly. "It was pure hell. I was 11 years old, with a developing body that all the guys made sure to point out to me on a daily basis. I was in a new school, with new people, and spent five days after school practicing cheerleading with five girls who had no intentions of getting to know me."

"Didn't you have your friends from your elementary school there to hang out with?" she asked.

"The school was so overcrowded, they taught in 'double sessions.' My elementary school friends went to the afternoon session, but since I was on the cheerleading team, I was sent to the morning session with all the other athletes. Most everyone I was in class with was new to me, yet they all knew each other. I hung out with the one or two kids from my elementary school I knew—all football players."

"And, of course, you probably got a lot of attention being the 'new' girl."

"Oh yes, then there was that." I did not smile. I remember it well.

"I was a size 3/4 but with a 36-inch chest. I could never get button-up shirts to actually button up, so I often wore cotton T-shirts, which just made it worse. There was this one boy who every day would grab at me while I was going up or down the long seventh-grade staircase. His name was Timmy something. One day I was going down the stairs as he was going up, and he grabbed my crotch. I was never prepared for where he was going to touch me. If I kept my books low below my belt, he would grab my breasts. If I kept them high up to my chest, it was my crotch.

"Anyway, this time one of the big football players, who coincidentally was in my next class, was behind me when it happened. ET saw the trauma I endured, and I will forever be grateful to him."

"And what did Mr. ET do to earn your gratitude?"

"It's funny because ET was this gentle giant. He never really spoke too much, but he always had such a pleasant way about him. We would say hi when we saw each other in the hall. And he was in my Social Studies class. We were friendly to each other. But that day, when Timmy —whatever his last name was—grabbed me, ET witnessed the incident.

"I'm not sure what he did to him, but when I got to class, ET came up to me and said, 'You won't have to worry about Timmy anymore.'"

"What did he mean?" Dr. H made a note.

"I don't know, but I heard that ET had a 'talk' with him. Whatever he said, he was right. After that day Timmy never bothered me again."

"I think we've gone off subject," she gently nudged me back on track.

"Perhaps it's my defense mechanism," I offered, thinking, *But I'm painting a picture.* "Looking back, I realize the cheerleaders shunning of me started before school, because we had a weeklong cheerleading camp in North Georgia before we started back to school in September. That's when I felt the snub.

"There were two girls in particular who were mean to me: Tess and Betty, but the ringleader was Tess. She was what I now know to be a fucking bitch. She was all of 12 and so conceited; it was *her* friend who didn't make the squad. She blamed me for getting the spot that rightfully, according to Tess, belonged to her friend."

"How were the other girls to you?"

"They were okay; I mean I did hang out with some of them sometimes. But they all had a lot of other friends; I felt alone. After all, when all of your friends you went through six years of elementary school with aren't around anymore; and then you have two hours after school of cheerleading practice; you really don't have time to devote to making new friends. And then I had my homework and schoolwork; I had to maintain my A average. I was so miserable. I felt awkward and not in control, and I was a fake at home. My parents thought I was this perfect child because to them, at home, I was. But at school, I was an outcast. And I was too embarrassed to let them know about my situation.

"I remember how the cheerleaders would always make plans to do other things during practice and never include me or ask me to join."

"Do you think you were oversensitive to this?"

"You mean, was it all in my mind?"

"Something like that."

"No, it wasn't." I remembered it well. "In fact, it was so obvious at the summer camp that our cheerleading coach actually had a meeting with the girls when we returned to Jonesboro and told them they were excluding me and reminded them that I was a part of the team and that they needed to remember that."

"So the coaches realized it?"

"Even before I did. I thought, *Maybe I'm being oversensitive*. Or, *Maybe I am feeling sorry for myself*. But it was obvious to everyone. Finally, one of their friends told me that they had wanted Tina to make the team and that's why they treated me the way they did."

"But you said not all the girls treated you badly."

"Well, when you're 11 and the only friends you hang out with don't talk to you at practice or include you in any activities, it is very obvious. They had to hang out with me, but they didn't have to go out of their way to be nice."

"Can you give me a solid example of something they did that was mean other than making you feel like an outsider?"

"*Lady Sings the Blues*," I said.

"The movie?" she asked.

"Yes. Very apropos don't you think?"

"I guess the significance will have to wait . . . perhaps we will need another double session." She made a note then waited for my response, which didn't come.

I smiled and took my leave. And for once I couldn't wait to come back for my next scheduled appointment and tell her the story of just how mean teen girls can be. How feelings from childhood can hang over your adult life like a web, entangling you, keeping you in a place of insecurity.

Chapter 7
Girl Sings the Blues

"If I had to define cruelty, I would use this as an example," I began my session.

I was casual that day—well, for me. I was wearing a long-sleeved Michael Kors shift dress in a navy herringbone pattern, MK chunky gladiator sandals in a saddle shade with matching belt and minimal jewelry. It was still winter, but in the South that can be 74 degrees and sunshine. My mood was as casual as my dress. I do not think it was a coincidence.

I dove right in.

"I had been secretly miserable for most of the school year. My parents had no clue as to my suffering. They didn't know the girls I spent the majority of my spare time with treated me with such coldness. They didn't know that I would cry myself to sleep. That I felt alone, different, and unpopular in a school of three hundred students where I was one of the 'chosen ones.' They didn't know this because I was too proud to let them know their 'golden child' was anything but."

I paused and took a can of Pamplemousse LaCroix out of my never-full LV bag, popped open the top, and took a sip of my water.

"But this one day, I was excited. It was a Friday, maybe it was October or March—I do not recall. I do recall that it was a blustery day; that weird time of the year when one day would be sunny and the next cold and windy. That's fall and spring in the South. Anyway, at cheerleading practice the girls were talking about going to the movies that night at the little Jonesboro theater. They were going to meet at seven p.m. for the movie *Lady Sings the Blues*. I listened to them as they discussed it, and then it happened. Tess turns to me and says, 'You can come, right?' I was beside myself. This was the first time I had been invited to join them when they made weekend plans.

"I had a bounce in my step when my mother picked me up from school that day. I told her all the cheerleaders were meeting at the theater to see the movie. Of course, that called for a new outfit, so we went to the store—Rich's, I think. I picked out a khaki-colored overall jumpsuit." I saw the look in her eyes.

"I know, but it was in style in 1972." I still shuddered at some of the things I used to wear in the name of fashion.

"No, it's not that," she explained. "I'm not questioning your fashion sense. Heaven knows I've never seen you in the same outfit twice, and we have been meeting like this for, what, seven months?"

"Nine," I told her.

"Right, nine. And in these nine months it's been like a fashion show, every time. I'm just in shock how you can recall what you wore forty years ago. I can't remember what I wore four days ago." She was smiling as she said this, and it gave me a glimpse into her kind demeanor.

"It's a curse; photographic memory. I replay my life, good and bad, over and over in my mind. Which is probably why I have so much trouble sleeping. Carrie Bradshaw said it best, ironically, in the *Sex and the City* episode revolving around her going to see a psychiatrist: 'I'm an emotional cutter.'"

"Emotional cutting?" she asked.

"Yes, emotional cutting, intentionally seeking out the things you know will hurt you; as in facing the truth," I explained.

"I'm sorry, it's now me who has taken you off track. Please, continue with your story."

"Right. So, Mother and Daddy take me to the local theater, hand me money, and watch me as I buy my ticket. I am the first one there. I purchase my ticket and find out what time the movie ends and go back to the car so I can tell them when to pick me up. They insist on waiting with me until the others arrive, but I assure them I will be okay and will wait inside for the other girls; then we would all sit together and watch the movie.

"I wave goodbye to my parents and tell them I will see them at nine p.m. when the movie is out. I buy popcorn and a Coke and wait in the lobby for the cheerleaders. By seven-twenty, when the movie is supposed to start, I am still the only one there. I wait until I hear the previews stop and when the movie begins, I go into the theater and look for them in the dark. Not one of the cheerleaders is there. I find a seat in the back row and sit by myself as I watch *Lady Sings the Blues*. They never came. Not one of them ever showed up."

"How traumatic that must have been for you," she said.

"Yes, very." I said as I remembered how it felt sitting in the dark movie theater alone. "I don't really remember much about the movie other than it starred Diana Ross and Billy Dee Williams. I remember the haunting music of Billie Holiday. I remember sitting in a dark theater by myself, an 11-year-old cheerleader with straight As and no friends. I remember feeling sorry for myself, paralyzed that someone from my school would see me sitting in that back row, watching a movie on a Friday night, alone.

"When it was over, I got up and walked straight out into the night and there were my parents, sitting in the car waiting on me. I got in the car; they asked me how I liked the movie. I told them it was OK and made idle chatter all the way home. I never told them that none of the other girls showed up, that I sat in the movie by myself, crying as I watched. I was too embarrassed to let them know."

"That must have seemed like a lifetime of waiting," she offered.

"It was, but it was a defining moment that really changed me for the rest of my life."

"How so?"

"It was that moment that I vowed never to be mean. Not that I was, but I would make a conscious effort to go forward in kindness to those around me. To make sure to say kind words, words of encouragement that will uplift a person, because you never know what people are going through."

"That really made quite an impact on you," she said, then added, "And that's a powerful lesson to learn at 11."

"Yes, very powerful, and like I said, it was a defining moment for me, I admit."

"What did you do when you went back to school on Monday?" she asked. "How did you react to the girls?"

"That was the hardest part, going back to school on Monday, facing the unknown. But I went back there, and I never breathed a word. I didn't tell them I went to the theater, I never mentioned I was there by myself, never asked them why they didn't come. I acted as if nothing happened."

"Do you think they knew?"

"I really don't know. It was never mentioned. I guess most girls would have come to practice and asked them what happened. I do not know why I didn't." *Pride*, I think to myself. *Pure Southern Baptist pride, that good old sweeping-the-bad-under-the-rug thing.*

"Did you have the urge to get back at them? I would think that would have been a natural response."

"I did get back at them."

"How?"

"Silently."

"Explain."

"It's my *9 ½ Weeks*—that awakening. Like Kim Basinger . . . it was the first time I used it, my power, I mean. It was in response to that 'mean girls' moment. I was 11, almost 12 years old, and the power was intoxicating."

She shifted in her chair, and I noticed that she was wearing suntan panty-hose, a shade too dark. "But what exactly do you mean?"

"Do you recall the proverbial saying: 'Revenge is a dish best served cold'?"

"*La vengeance est un plat qui se mange froid*," she said fluently.

"I'm impressed," and I was. "Well, I realized that the only reason all the girls were jealous of me was because of the way their boyfriends acted around me. I picked up on this right away. The funny thing was I wasn't interested in their boyfriends. I valued their friendship way more than I did the attention of their boyfriends. But that all changed after that movie night. It was a 'game-changer' so to speak."

"In what way?"

I laughed. "I liken it to the movie *Carrie*, when she realizes she has this power and then harnesses it when she needs to. I learned that I can turn my power on and off."

"What do you mean by power?" She was interested. I could tell by the way she sat on the edge of her chair, pen in hand.

"I didn't really know what it was. I only knew that if I was around a boy and looked at him in a certain way, then I could get my way. It was quite comical to me, actually, and quite by accident that I discovered there could be this dance between boys and a girl. With my newfound knowledge, I decided to test my theory out."

"Test it out on whom?"

"On the boyfriends of the cheerleaders on my squad." I responded.

"Go on," she implored.

She waited for the story. I didn't disappoint her as I traveled below the surface, like she requested, underneath the cold hard ice that had kept me afloat for far too long.

And I did. Offering an explanation of how trophy wives, like me, come to be.

Chapter 8

Mean Girls

"It was the end of the school year of 1973, some months after the movie incident—like I said, best served cold. That was the moment when I knew I would close the book on what was a very bitter chapter in my oh-so-young life. I didn't realize then how deeply that seventh-grade year would affect me. I suffered in silence and pretended all was well, when in fact I was crying internally daily. I look back and can see how those nine months of being shunned, ignored, bullied . . . how that school year helped to shape me, good or bad, into the person I would eventually become."

I paused and thought about how I hide behind fashion as a way of coping. Always in style, always on point. The right dress, the right bag, the right shoes. All on the surface, no going deep beyond the exterior. Until now.

"And how are you different because of that year?" Dr. H asked.

"I made a vow, much like Scarlet did with the red clay of Tara in her hand, that I would never purposely be mean to anyone. That I would see everyone's worth. No one should be made to feel like an outcast, as if they did not matter. It's true what they say, you know, that in the end only kindness matters."

"Again, that's an important lesson learned at a very early age," she replied. "Do you think you made the right decision to suffer in silence?"

"Who knows?" I responded. "It has made me who I am today, I know that much. Besides, I don't look back. Well, at least not until now, with you. I remember an interview I saw late one night in New York when I couldn't sleep. I have always had trouble falling to sleep. Anyway, I was flipping through channels, and I came across an interview with Dolly Parton, whom I had just met the day before when Bill, my third husband, was interviewing the trio: Dolly, Emmylou Harris, and Linda Ronstadt. The interviewer asked Dolly what was the worst mistake she ever made? Ms. Parton responded, and I paraphrase: 'I haven't made *any* mistakes.' After the hosts laughed at her statement, she said, 'Now wait.' Then she went on to explain that every decision she has made was the right decision for her at that time. She said she could look back on things and see where maybe it wasn't the best decision, but she chooses not to. Not to look back and say, *Well, that wasn't right for me, now was it?* Because at that particular time, she thought it was the right decision. That way of thinking was life-altering for me. I can look back and see where I was wrong in my choices, my decisions, but why? We all try to do what's best or right at the time. Hindsight is 20/20, but why beat yourself up about past failures?

"I know what you're thinking, Doctor," I added.

"And what is that, Lisa?"

"If I suffered in silence as a child, could that be the reason I was able to suffer in silence as an adult? Was it the reason I stayed too long in bad relationships or abusive marriages? Who knows? It taught me to be patient with people who don't like me based on first impressions—and there have been many over the years. I remember when I was in one of those first PR roles I told you about. The one where I met Mike, the father of my girls. Again, I was all of 24 years old and was the head of the public information department for the county. Of course, I was the only one in the department," I said, laughing.

"Anyway, I was in charge of getting all the public information brochures printed, and I drove over to meet the longtime printer who had the contract with the county. It was a husband-wife-son team who were very old-school. She was cool and aloof to me at first, but I kept being nice and would take them cookies or a cake or some small token each time I went to their office.

"Finally, one day she said to me, 'Lisa, I want to apologize to you.' I asked why and she said: 'I misjudged you. I thought you were going to be stuck-up and hard to deal with. A prima donna. But you are one of the nicest people I have ever worked with. I am sorry that my first impression of you was wrong and that I treated you badly based on it.'

"Funny thing was, I was so used to people treating me in that manner that it didn't even register. I learned to adapt. I guess I learned it by watching my mother. She was this mythical creature—so beautiful, kind, and smart.

"Mother was also so strong and graceful—after all, her name is Grace. I watched and learned from her." I paused.

"Well, your parents are the two tallest trees in your forest," replied Dr. H, "and everything you learn stems from the shadow they cast over your life." She was writing something in her book.

"That's a very visual statement. I can see how that works in your psych-speak of trying to sort through people's lives. Is that why I try to disarm and charm people?"

"In all probability, yes," she answered. "We have yet to broach your seventh-grade cheerleader revenge." She, once again, put me back on track.

"I know, let me guess, our time is up."

"Almost," she said, putting a finger in the air and motioning for me to start the story.

"It's a short story," I said. "It was the end of seventh grade, and I knew I would be changing schools. Remember how I said the reason we were in double sessions was because there were too many students? Well, the Board of Education was in the process of redrawing school district lines. The girls I spent most of my time with would be going to a different school than me, so I would not be dealing with them much longer.

"There was an 'end of school' party at the lake house belonging to one of the guys' parents—I never had problems being invited to parties by the guys, just the girls—so I went. Guess who else was there? All the girls who had been mean to me. That's when I decided to test out my newfound theory."

"Which was?"

"Getting guys to do things for me by"—I paused—"I think it's called 'flirting,'" I said sarcastically.

"I spent the next two hours getting each one of the girls' boyfriends to leave them to get me something. A drink, a napkin, Cheetos—it didn't matter what it was; it was the fact that, one by one, they left their girlfriends and followed me to the kitchen or the pool room."

"You realize what they were thinking, right?"

"Slut, whore, bitch . . . I am sure. But I didn't care. And I was amazed at how easy it was. I just cut my eyes, made a statement like: 'I wonder where the kitchen is?' and whichever guy was my target jumped up and offered to show me. The girls were furious."

"I recall you saying that was the year you learned to be nice to everyone?" she inquired in her nonjudgmental way.

"It was," I answered. "But it was also the year I learned why."

"And how did it feel?" she asked. "Getting back at the 'mean girls'?"

"Not as good as I thought it would," I answered. "I was young and hurt and wanted to hurt them back. I guess revenge is not all it's cracked up to be. I find that I am better at being kind. In the end, killing your enemies with kindness may take longer, but it is much more satisfying."

Chapter 9
Wild Horses

It was raining in Georgia that afternoon, and I almost canceled my appointment. I said as much to Dr. H as I took off my soaking wet, black hooded raincoat. It's the one I bought on the streets in Paris when Bill and I got caught in a summer rainstorm.

I had pulled my long golden-brown tresses into a sleek ponytail. By the end of the day, my hair would be swollen from the Southern humidity, as well as my feet from all the salted margaritas I drank the night before with my youngest group of girlfriends—not the "ladies who lunch" set, but the rowdy ones who do not have kids or husbands, therefore they do not have to hurry home to homework or housework. I am no longer allowed to drink margaritas, per my friends and family, but some days with certain friends, tequila was my only option.

"Well, I'm glad you didn't," she responded.

It had been two weeks since I'd been to her office, and I was, in a way, glad to be back on the blue denim couch. Our routine was different now. Our sessions, having progressed to bi-monthly, which I took as a sign of improvement on my part, were more relaxed. I was starting to feel the security of this room and its occupant, even if I wanted to redo the entire decor, starting with the blue and white ticking fabric throw pillow I was cradling in my arms.

"Did I ever tell you that I received an 'A' on my screenplay from my Emory professor. I'm curious what grade you would have given me if you were judging?" I asked with a smile.

"I pass no judgments," she said, probably thinking I was serious, when, in fact, I was being playful. "I will never grade you on your feelings."

Did she understand that I was being sarcastic and wasn't playing along, or did she not have it in her to color outside the lines? I dropped the thought and handed her a book.

"What's this?" She put on her reading glasses. They are faux tortoise shell in the same style as her red readers, "Oh, *The Joy of Sex*. I wasn't even born when this book came out, but I remember reading about all the controversy. It was 1971, if I'm not mistaken."

"1972," I corrected her.

"*The Joy of Sex* is an illustrated sex manual by British author Alex Comfort, M.B., Ph.D., first published in 1972," she was reading the front cover. "What does this mean to you?"

"I first found a copy of it in Mother and Daddy's bedroom when I was 14," I explained. "I found this copy at a flea market over the weekend, and it triggered another memory."

"And you needed this information at 14 because . . .?" She didn't finish her thought, leaving me with a copious opportunity and space to answer.

In fact, she always paused just a bit too long, enough so that I felt there was this awkward, lingering span of space that I needed to fill, dead air waiting for words, overcompensating for the silence as if it were my fault.

Just like my mother.

It reminded me of all the times I would accompany her on shopping trips to Rich's department store, along with her "returning" trips, as I called them, to take back the merchandise Daddy deemed unnecessary. Rich's was a familiar stage in my life. It was where our Sunday clothes were purchased; it was where we would go visit Santa (when he didn't come to our house), and where we searched for the perfect gift or outfit to match whatever occasion or event we were attending—weddings, baby showers, funerals.

It was also where I learned that my mother made apologies for everything—never placing blame on anyone but herself for having to return an item of clothing. She couldn't just return an item and say nothing, or admit: "I have to return this because my husband found the Rich's bill I hid from him, and he's making me bring this back." After all, what would people think? No, her returns were always accompanied by long, drawn-out explanations like, "I didn't realize I had a dress very similar to this one already in my closet, so there's really no use in keeping them both, is there?" Or "I thought these shoes would match an outfit I purchased at Finale on Five last season, but the shade was just a little bit off—more ruby red than the garnet I needed."

No one who worked at Rich's, whether 17 or 70, cared why she was bringing back the merchandise. Yet she felt a need to let them know the reason, to apologize, as if she were offending them for not keeping the pink and red caftan that she bought because she thought it made her look like Elizabeth Taylor, when Daddy told her she looked more like Mama Cass. "What were you thinking?" my dad asked when he saw the gown hanging in the closet.

It was during one of the return episodes when I discovered the book. She handed me a Rich's bag and asked me to go to her closet and pack up a color-block pantsuit: "I just don't think it's the right fit for me." The pants had fallen off the hanger onto the floor of her side of the closet, so I got down on my knees to pick them up. When I did, I accidentally knocked off the top of a large Etienne Aigner shoe box. And there it was, *The Joy of Sex*. I hesitated when I saw the word *sex*, as all of its taboos instantly swirled in my mind. Coupled with the word *joy*, it was the exact opposite of what we were taught in Bible school, the "sins of the flesh" and all. It was almost like a perfect oxymoron, much like "jumbo shrimp" or "adult male."

I hastily put the top back on the box—guess that cat was out of the bag—and brought back the item I was sent to retrieve. But when the coast was clear, which it was every Tuesday and Thursday when mother ran her errands, I would sneak up to her room with a flashlight, slide open the closet door, take a seat on her pile of shoes, close the door gently, and read from *The Joy of Sex*, unnoticed by the others who were outside playing.

"I read it without their knowledge, of course," I confessed. "That's how I learned, at the age of 14, the proper way to give a blow job. It was also the age I lost my virginity."

"That's so young," she said without a trace of judgment in her tone. "Was this a traumatic event for you?"

"Not compared to the rest of my sexual history up to that point," I responded dryly.

"I was in ninth grade," I started. "I was a cheerleader, and most of my time was spent with the other cheerleaders at practice, at games, at sleepover parties. I was a teenager, that's what you did. You really didn't have a boyfriend *per se*. I had crushes and kisses, but it was a time—an age of innocence, if you will—that made life easy and unencumbered."

"But you had already been molested by your father's friends by then," Dr. H looked up from her notepad, a bit confused by my last statement.

"Yes, but they were *men*. I was hanging out with 14-year-old boys who were afraid of me," I laughed. "I could just be a 14-year-old girl around other 14-year-olds."

How did she not see that? How could anyone not see that I could compartmentalize my persona? I am a Gemini, a twin. And I was a good, Southern Baptist "it girl" with a 4.0 grade point average, an excellent student with tons of girlfriends; I was the one child my parents didn't have to worry about or pay to get good grades. I just did what I was supposed to do, and it made life so much easier on me than my sisters. Jennifer was always breaking the rules, and Kim just didn't bother to follow them. But then, there was the other side of me: the girl who asked for slinky nightgowns and marabou slippers; the girl who would dance all alone in her bedroom with imagined boyfriends; the girl who would stare in the mirror, trying to see exactly what it was that made her different.

"I was in ninth grade, and one of my teachers, Mr. Locke, asked if he could see me after class. Of course, I stayed after everyone else left, wondering if I had done something wrong. When he asked me, point blank, why I didn't have a boyfriend, I told him I didn't know. Mr. Locke was my Social Studies teacher, but he was also head of the Y Clubs, and he held a contest to raise money for the club. He asked me if a date with me could be the prize for the boy who raised the most money.

Because I always had a hard time saying *no*—"If you're not going to eat your lunch, can I have it?" Or "Even though you're not invited to my party because my boyfriend thinks you're cute, can I borrow the outfit you would have worn?"—I told him yes. I agreed to be the "prize." All of the eighth and ninth grade boys started raising money to win a date with me to the school dance. Some members of the football team threatened that they were raising money to give to the nerdiest boy in school, so he could win the date."

I smiled at this memory. I had almost forgotten about the contest for a date with me as the prize. Some prize I was now.

"What happened?" she asked.

"I guess I'm getting ahead of myself. Let me go back to Mr. Locke's question," I replied as I pulled out a bottle of Perrier from my black Prada purse (a gift from my last husband) and took a sip. "After Mr. Locke asked me if I had a boyfriend, he explained that he wanted to set me up with one of his favorite former students . . . that the guy was dating another girl, but he thought I would be perfect for him."

"That sounds a bit unusual," she chimed in.

"You have no idea," I laughed nervously. "Turns out, the former student, MD, was a senior at the high school. He was a star on the basketball team and had a longtime girlfriend, also a senior and the star on the girls' basketball team, whom everyone thought he would marry, including her."

"It's the beginning of a pattern," Dr. H said.

I couldn't tell if she was talking to me or to herself, but she made a note in her book and looked up at me to let me know she was really listening.

"He was 18. I was 14, but I looked older. Mr. Locke arranged for us to meet one day after school. The next thing I knew, he had broken up with his girlfriend and started dating me." I reflected on the year we met, 1975, and flashed back to our first date.

"The first time he took me out, we went to a movie. I'd never been on a date and had no expectations for the evening. MD came to the house on Edgewood Way and met my parents. Of course, they were impressed by his looks, his manners, his car. We left and went to dinner at an Italian restaurant up the street before the movies. We saw *Tommy*, though I wanted to see *The Stepford Wives*. That should have told me something. Anyway, he brought me home; it was about nine-thirty p.m. He walked me to the door, I kissed him goodnight and went inside, leaving him on the porch.

"When I walked in, my parents were sitting in the formal living room waiting on me. They asked where he was, and I told them he left. Then Mother asked, 'You didn't invite him in?' I didn't know to do that. It was funny and very telling that I had not been schooled in the art of dating."

"But you weren't a typical 14-year-old?" This time it *was* a question.

"In hindsight, no. I was very mature for my age, intellectually and socially. I remember finding a Jacqueline Susann novel at one of the houses where I was babysitting. It was *Once Is Not Enough*. When the woman came home and saw me reading it, she called my mother to see if it was okay. . . " I trailed off at the memory and paused to give Dr. H time to comment on what I thought should be perfect fodder for any therapist.

"I guess, if you're dating an 18-year-old man who had a steady girlfriend before you, the subject of sleeping together would naturally come up." I laughed out loud at the pun. But she didn't notice, or maybe she just didn't appreciate my sense of humor.

"Of course, our make-out sessions soon became very steamy. So, during the summer of my fourteenth year, I lost my virginity to my 18-year-old boyfriend." I said it matter-of-factly, with a shrug as if to say, "What's the big deal?"

"How did you feel?" she asked. "After the fact?"

"For me, it was just painful. There wasn't passion or longing. I wasn't experienced enough to understand that part of sex yet. For him, it was all about release. I'm guessing, of course. But for me, it was uncomfortable, something you did because he wanted to." I paused and thought about my prior sexual experiences. Although none involved the total penetration of intercourse, the feelings were the same in some ways. Whether someone was sticking their tongue down your throat at the age of four, or their finger up your vagina while touching your breast at the age of eleven, it was still a distinct, awkward invasion of your being. And yet, in my fucked-up reality, it sent a signal to my brain that I was special because someone wanted me.

"So, why did you explore the book?" Dr. H lifted up the copy of *The Joy of Sex* (circa 1972) in her hand.

"Ah yes, the book. I was curious about the book because MD asked me to perform oral sex on him, and I wanted to know about it. It just so happened that I was in my parents' room, found the book, and started looking into it. There were illustrations on how to pleasure a man. In hindsight, the lessons turned out to be very helpful."

"How do you mean?" she asked.

"When I executed or put into practice what I had read from the book and performed the act on him the first time, he was amazed. He asked me where I learned how to do it so well, and I told him that I read it in a book. I often wondered why what I did was so different, but turns out, I'm *really* good at giving a blow job."

"Do you think it's because you have a high level of the desire to please?"

"No. I think it's because I'm a good reader, and readers are leaders!" I was making another joke, but she didn't think this one was funny either.

"I want you to consider that your sexuality was awakened unnaturally . . . that a lot of your issues, in addition to the need to please men, stem from your mother's expectations and your early molestations."

"I have considered it," I said. "And it begs the question, am I sexually active because of my early molestations? Or was I molested because I am, by nature, a sexual creature?"

"I think you know where I stand on this issue," she stated matter-of-factly. "You are not to blame for what happened to you at such a young age."

"Well, I learned to have an orgasm and enjoy sex, and I do *not* regret that."

"Did you experience your first orgasm with your first boyfriend?"

"Yes, it was quite by accident. But when it happened, it changed everything. I went from having sex to please my boyfriend, to enjoying it for myself. Plus, it opened up a whole new aspect to loving someone."

"And were there any problems in the relationship? Was it a healthy, positive one?" Dr. H asked.

"I would say so, yes, in most ways it was. But how healthy can a relationship be when there's that much distance between age and experience?" I replied. "We were never in the same school; I was in ninth grade at the junior high and he was a twelfth grader at the senior high. He was my first love, but I felt more like a possession to him. I realized that he loved me more than I loved him; I was incapable of giving real love at that age. He kept tabs on me when we were apart. He did introduce me to Jimmy Buffet and The Rolling Stones; he wined and dined me at the Midnight Sun, Moonraker, and The Coach & Six; but he also introduced me to the concept of jealousy. I don't regret the relationship and all of the perks that went with it. I was there to support him. And although he was there to support me, too, there were some drawbacks to being with him."

"How was that?" she asked.

"Because he knew, and I knew, our relationship was the reason I didn't make the high school cheerleading team the summer before I went into tenth grade. It turned out that the cheerleading coach and the girls' basketball coach were one in the same."

"And you were dating the ex-boyfriend of the star player of the girls' basketball team," Dr. H surmised.

"Yes. I should have known that I wouldn't make the cut. But my positive outlook and never-give-up attitude led me into a false security; one that assured me that the fact I'd taken her boyfriend away from her wouldn't matter." (How naive was I? Yes, I was only 14, but I didn't just steal her boyfriend. I was also fucking him.)

"But it did," she said.

I simply answered, "Yes, it did."

There were thirty girls going out for the varsity squad that had three openings and a junior varsity team that had six spots. After tryouts, we gathered *en masse* and were instructed to go home and wait. Tradition was that you would be notified if you made the team that evening; the current cheerleaders would pile into a van and drive to your house to let you know, in person, that you were chosen, and for which squad. Thinking back, it was a very cruel way of notifying someone. A symbolic form of aggregation, archaic in theory and practice. I went straight home from school and began the wait. MD came over (it was a Friday after all) and spent the long night of wondering with me.

We waited until well after midnight. MD had to leave, because he was tired and he had to attend basketball camp first thing in the morning. I, too, said I was tired and would be heading to bed, but it was a lie. I walked him to the door with an awkward goodbye; he knew I didn't make the team, and in my heart, so did I. But I stayed up after he left, looking out my window in great expectation of hearing the sound of a van, filled with cheerleaders, coming to my door to tell me I was chosen. But they never came.

I finally looked at the clock; it read three a.m. The moon shone down on our driveway, making the emptiness of it all the more clear. There would be no cheer van pulling into the open space, no knock on my door, no handing me the FPSH Cheerleader T-shirt I was supposed to wear the following Monday to announce to the entire school that I had made the team.

I was not chosen.

"How could that be?" my mother asked the next morning. "You have been cheering since you were 5!" I felt her disappointment wash over me in waves. She did the math, just like I did late last night, as I was staring out my bedroom window into the darkness—grade point average, 4.0; teacher recommendations, all exceptional; all the right boxes checked off perfectly.

But I knew the reason (the real one) why I didn't make the team, though I never told Mother. It was then, in my fourteenth year, I was forced into the realization that every choice you make has a consequence. Every single one.

I also realized, after the very public display of not becoming a high school cheerleader, that it wasn't the end of the world—that I would survive this disappointment, as well as every disappointment that would follow.

But most importantly, I learned that giving a proper blow job could make or break a relationship.

I left Dr. H's office and went straight home to download "Wild Horses" by the Stones. I listened to the song the rest of the day on repeat, remembering those times when life was not as cruel or complicated. I thought about Jacqueline Susann's January Wayne character and the camel wool coat I had to have after seeing the movie. I found my mind going back to the day, months after my rejection from the cheerleading team, that Mother bought a camel-colored coat similar to the one I so desperately wanted. She had it lovingly displayed on my bed when I came home from school. I savored the memory and stayed in that moment, wrapped in the cold comfort of a cashmere coat, until my mind, succumbing to the warmth, finally let go and allowed a deep sleep to take over.

Chapter 10

Nowhere Road

There was a different scent wafting in the air as I took my usual seat on the denim couch next to Dr. H's brown leather chair. I made a mental note to see what candle she was burning before I left her office that day. It was not a pleasant scent, by any means, but one that hung around the room like an uninvited guest standing on your front porch awkwardly waiting to be asked to stay.

"I must say, you are looking very sharp in your Chanel," she complimented me. "You must have another appointment after ours!"

Unable to decide if she was fishing for insight into my day or if she was genuinely interested in why I was wearing Chanel for a doctor's appointment, I was actually impressed that she recognized the designer. And I was *decked out* in Chanel: a black and winter white houndstooth tweed suit from a collection a few years back, but I was sure she didn't know this. My classic black quilted Chanel purse with interlocking Cs and my cream pumps with black patent leather toes, which were all on point. I was even wearing my mother's favorite perfume—Chanel N°5. I had a ladies-who-lunch date with my socialite friends at the club. So, this must have been a Thursday.

I handed her my poem, "Nowhere Road."

Looking back I can see the sunlight streaking though the trees that covered the land where you lived…

And I remember early mornings of waffles in the iron and laughter in the air-

And I, dressed in Easter white, witnessed the sun touch your hair and I knew then that you were truly golden.

And my world would be measured by these sun streaked days and starry, starry nights when life was young and unburdened.

Dr. H read my work, then placed the poem in her lap and silently waited for me to begin the session.

"There was a girl on my dorm hall my freshman year of college at the University of Georgia," I said. "Her name was Bella, and she was absolutely the most beautiful girl I had ever seen in person. She was tall and thin, with natural blonde hair that fell perfectly and greener eyes than mine. We went through sorority rush together, and I couldn't understand why she was cut from every sorority, even the less popular ones.

"I wanted to befriend her because I noticed she didn't seem to have many friends, but all the other girls in my hall discouraged me. They said she had a bad reputation. So I watched in wonder as guy after guy would come to take her out—a different one every night. And I thought, wow, she has a date every night of the week. But then I noticed that they would never come back, never a repeat date. She was a one-time girl, a one-night stand. . .

"I haven't thought of her in years," I sighed. "She didn't last through the first quarter. She had a total breakdown, and her parents had to come pick her up in the middle of the night. I watched as they wrapped a blanket around her fragile frame and walked her down the hall. I never saw her again, but I remember it so vividly."

"Why is this so important to you?" Dr. H finally broke her silence.

"Because she was my only witness."

"Witness to what?

I took the bottle of water set before me on the glass-topped table and paused for a moment while I took a sip. I wasn't thirsty; I was just trying to decide whether I wanted to continue down this road, a road I knew would lead to a very painful story—my story—the one I have never spoken about to anyone in almost thirty years.

"It was my senior year of high school," I began. "I was dating a guy; let's call him Will. He was older than me, of course. I was 18 and he was 26, I think. He had a medical background and drove a Cadillac. He sent me flowers every week and took me to the newest restaurants in Atlanta. I guess you could say he wined and dined me. I didn't really even like him that much, but I liked all the attention and the gifts; it was a way of passing time until I left for college."

"Why were you dating someone so much older than you again? Why not someone in your high school?" Dr. H interrupted with another question.

"I never dated anyone in my high school," I said. "Unless coaches count." I was kidding, of course, but the look on her face told me she believed me. I continued.

"I never dated anyone in my high school, because no one in school ever asked me out," I explained. *Isn't this where I left off the last time?* "Daddy told me that his golfing buddy, who had a son in my class, told him no one ever asked me out because I only dated older guys." I found this funny and laughed out loud. "Is that considered irony?" I always confused the meaning, much like Alanis Morissette.

"Will sent flowers to our home every week, gave me my first emerald. Many times before we had a date, he would give me his credit card to buy a new outfit; told me to sign it Mrs. whatever his last name was, which I did a few times. But I knew that I was getting ready to leave home for college, and

I didn't want to lead him on. I liked him, but I wasn't *in love* with him, or not as much in love as he was with me.

It became quite uncomfortable, the difference in our feelings. I realized this and tried to distance myself, but the more I tried to let go, the harder he held on. It was early August; I was preparing to head to the University of Georgia's sorority rush when he surprised me with a platinum and diamond ring. And then, to my utter shock, he actually asked me to marry him. That's when I knew it was over for me. I couldn't pretend any longer. And I couldn't lead him on. He cried when I said no and broke up with him instead."

I took another sip of my water, trying to place the scent of the burning candle, but my mind could not for the life of me determine the fragrance. It distracted and sickened me all at once.

"While I prepared for college, Will called me and asked if he could take me out one last time before I left for Athens. My parents were away that weekend, and I was supposed to be keeping an eye on my younger sister, Kim. Jennifer was married and out of the house by then. He knew I had been wanting to go to The Ambassador restaurant in Atlanta, so that's where he told me he would take me. There was something inside that told me to say no, a small voice I would later learn to listen to. But against my better judgement, I agreed to go to dinner with him this one last time.

"He wanted to pick me up from my house, but I insisted on meeting him at his apartment so I could have some element of control. He had champagne chilled for me when I arrived. We had a nice conversation on the way to the restaurant. I remember because I was concerned it would be awkward since, in my mind, this would be the last time I would see him.

"We arrived at the restaurant on Piedmont Road, past old homes that gave way to strip malls of nondescript white buildings that had become more common in the late '70s. The Ambassador was set apart by grandiose green palms in bronze planters and twinkling lights that framed the doorway. Wearing my new oversized khaki pants, short-sleeved cream linen shirt with mother of pearl buttons, and gray and cream striped linen vest a la Annie Hall, I had a smoldering confidence in the evening that would never take root—a grown-up goodbye, if you will.

"We were seated at the 'best' table in the middle of The Ambassador's large dining room. Will ordered a bottle of Dom and, with a sly grin, toasted to my graduation. I took a sip. Then, another toast, this time to my new life. I raised my champagne coupe and reached out to touch his glass, but somewhere over the flowers, the bread basket, and the candle's yellow glow, the room became still, as if someone had pressed Pause.

"Try as I may, I don't remember hearing the clink of the glasses, only the hush that surrounded me. The rest of the evening was a total blank. I don't remember what I ordered for dinner, or if I even ate. If I laughed when he spoke, I couldn't say, for I have no recollection of our conversation. I don't remember walking out of the restaurant. *Nothing.* The candlelit champagne toast to new beginnings turned out to be my last memory of that evening."

I stopped. Took a very deep breath. Swallowed. I tried very hard not to hyperventilate at the memory that was welling up inside of me. Even now the thought of that night could make my heart race and my head spin out of control. *Control*—all these years of waiting to finally find that word.

"I woke up the next day in his bed. Naked, with my knees bent, and two pillows propped under my legs. Drowsy, confused, and somewhat bewildered by the position of my body—why were there pillows under my bent knees?—I sat up and looked for my clothes. The outfit I'd so carefully chosen (so as not to entice him), was crumpled on the hardwood floor of his bedroom next to the dresser. The linen pants, now more clown-like than billowy, were lined and creased from the movements of the night before. Maybe they recalled being removed from my body, because I surely didn't. I couldn't find my panties, so I put on my pants without them. The tiny mother of pearl buttons of my windowpane patterned shirt were now too small and hard to close. Yesterday I found them delicate and worth the extra effort to button; now they were slowing me down, a burden to my escape.

"I could hear him in the kitchen preparing breakfast, cabinets opening, utensils being moved, the sound of the refrigerator closing, as if this was just another day. I was the definition of 'dazed and confused,' and I was furious as I walked out of the bedroom, my tan Candies and vest in my hands. 'You drugged me!' I almost screamed the accusation at him, while he continued to make breakfast. I looked for my purse and ignored his assurances that I *wanted* to sleep with him one last time. My mind still hazy, I ran out of the apartment and drove the short distance home. As expected, I took a long, hot bath, as if anything could wash away the night before."

"So you were drugged and date-raped," she said with a concerned look, but not really surprised.

"I guess we can add that to my list," I said softly.

"Is this what you found difficult to write about, being raped?" she asked.

"The saddest part is that because I was drugged and don't remember anything that happened to me, I don't have any tangible feelings about being violated. I have no memory of anything. Not of going back to his apartment, or taking off my clothes, or sleeping with him." I exhaled and paused briefly, as I forced the next confession. "But the story doesn't end there," I said, the sadness creeping back into my memory.

"I leave for rush the next week, an intense week of eating store-bought cookies and drinking pineapple juice cocktails with all the fake smiles, insincere niceties, the backstabbing that naturally occurs when you throw three hundred Southern girls from different backgrounds into a parade of first impressions and the ultimate game of 'pick me!' I made all the cuts, which were brutal for some, and pledged my sorority, Kappa Delta, with little time between the pageantry of college and the beginning of freshman classes.

"Six weeks after school started, I became very ill. Vomiting every morning and bouts of being nauseated all day. My Aunt Gail, who lives in Athens, was so concerned after she came to check on me that she took me to her house and nursed me back to health.

"It was 1979, the year Rely tampons came on the market and all the girls received a sample of the product in our dorm welcome packages. I don't know if you remember the story behind the tampons, but they were supposed to be revolutionary. They turned out to be toxic. The company ended up taking them off the market because they were proven to cause toxic shock syndrome."

"But you didn't have toxic shock syndrome, did you?" Dr. H interjected.

"No."

"What did you do next?"

"I went home and, as much as I hated to, I contacted Will. The bastard admitted he wanted to impregnate me so I would marry him instead of going to college. A nightmare come true."

"How did you feel about your options at the time?" she asked.

"There were no options!" I said emphatically. "I was not marrying him, and I was not going to keep a baby that I had no say whatsoever in making: one that was conceived after I was drugged and then raped. Besides, I was a freshman in college. I had prepared my entire life to get into UGA—studied hard, took all the college prep classes, made the drill team after my failed cheerleading tryouts, and was accepted into the National Honor Society on my way to the top. How dare he take that away from me?"

"So you had an abortion," she stated without posing a question.

"Yes. I had an abortion," I reflected on that word and let it linger a while. For so long it was whispered amid the good and the bad—among the girls who would have them and the boys who would pay for them. The scarlet A—a badge of shame, despair, carelessness. But then, as it would have been now, it was my only option.

"He made all the arrangements, and I made him buy a wedding ring for me to wear, as if that would take away some of the shame. I lied and gave my name as his wife at the clinic. When we were in consultation, I could barely stand to be in the same room with him, much less sit next to him and pretend we were married. I held the injustice of what he had done to me in my heart and over my entire being. I could feel its strength as readily as I could feel my pain. I wore it like a badge; it was my power play—the only thing I had left.

"The clinic counselor asked if we were 'OK' with our decision, and he had the nerve to say he was *not*. I couldn't contain my hatred for him. How dare he drug me, rape me, impregnate me, and then have *any* say whatsoever in my decision to abort. It was a harsh decision, but it was mine to make, not his. He already had his choice; now it was my choice."

The anger and rage boiled up inside of me like a pot of water waiting to be tamed. Just as it had in the fall of 1979. I suddenly realized I was yelling.

"Would you like to take a break?" Dr. H asked.

"No. I haven't spoken about this out loud to anyone, and I'm ready finally to close this chapter," I responded.

"I have the abortion. I go home to my parents' house and recover. Of course, they have no idea. They think I have TSS and are very attentive. I know I should feel ashamed, but instead I am angry. Maybe if I was careless. Maybe if I had a choice, or even remembered the night I conceived, I would have felt shame, but I didn't feel anything. Nor will I ever.

"I kept the paperwork from my procedure. I didn't want Will to have possession of anything related to that day, or to me. Afterward, I never saw, spoke to, or heard from him again. Nor did I have any desire to."

"And you didn't press charges?" she asked.

"No. That wasn't the mindset back then. It was an incestuous environment of 'good ole boys' being boys. 'Fuck frats' where sexual conquests were calculated on bed posts and belts. Where the goal was to get the 'nice' girls, the ones who sit home on weekends waiting for the phone call or the second date that never comes because the guy has moved on to the next new conquest. So no, I didn't press charges. Instead, I went back to Athens that Sunday as if nothing happened.

"Midterms were upon us, so I was up late studying. It was two in the morning when I decided to take a break."

I paused for a moment in my memory of that life-changing weekend and continued.

"No matter where I looked in my dorm room, my mind took me back to the envelope tucked between the books on my shelf. I decided there was only one way I could deal with the matter, not wanting to exert any more of my time on that one incident that I refused to let define me. I went to the bookshelf, took my clinic paperwork out of my Bible and The Ambassador matchbook I found in the bottom of my purse, and I headed down the hall to the communal bathroom of Brumby Hall. That's when I saw Bella being wrapped in a blanket and taken away by her parents."

"But I thought you said she was *your* witness?" Dr. H asked.

"She was; she was the only witness to me with my paperwork as I made my way down the hall. I think she saw the sadness in my eyes because she looked at me and mouthed: 'You'll be OK.' as they were carrying her off. She's being carted off in the middle of the night by her parents, yet I was the one with all the secrets.

"I watched as she left our hall for good and then walked into the large, white-tiled bathroom that every girl on our floor used. It was surprisingly clean, sterile, quiet, and cold. I stood in front of one of the white porcelain sinks (the second one on the right as you walked in the door, to be exact). I looked in the mirror at my 18-year-old self, then I got down on my knees, bowed my head, and prayed. I asked God to forgive me for what I had done, for my procedure. Then I got up off my knees, took the matches and lit the corner of my paperwork, holding it until it was engulfed in flames. I dropped the flaming paper into the sink and watched it burn until there was nothing left but charcoal embers. Turning on the faucets, I took note as the ashes circled the drain and were washed away, just like my sins were when I was baptized. And I never looked back," I said. "Until now."

Dr. H stared at me intently as if she was trying not to cry. But I was not crying; I had shed all the tears I had on this matter. It was what made me such a proponent for choice, the hard line in the drifting sands of time that I was determined to keep. And I firmly believe that no one should take away your choice, for it's just that, *yours.*

My mind drifted off to that damn scented candle and then it hit me. It was the smell of dark musk—it was the smell of *him.* It reminded me of bad cologne and forced decisions.

Chapter 11

In the Midnight Hour

We'd reached the point where our sessions played out to a particular rhythm. A certain cadence, much like the sound of the cicada when it first makes itself known. Quietly at first, then a symbol of sound progresses as it rises out of the ground. Then, just like that, it shrinks back down from whence it came. It was this rhythm of nothings, then breakthroughs, followed by release. Perhaps *this* would be considered progress, but I had nowhere else for *this* to go; I had hit rock bottom, but I found some light as I gradually climbed my way out of the hole I fell deep into, one memory at a time.

"No note for me today?" Dr. H asked as we took our usual seats.

"I'm sorry, no. Not today. I reconnected with my cousin, my father's first cousin to be exact. Tommy Roe. Yes, the singer." I responded to the look in her eyes. "He is married to a fabulous French woman, Josette Banzet, who happens to have been an actress in one of my favorite movies, *The Other Side of Midnight*. The movie came out in 1977, when I was in high school, and it had a profound effect on me. I watched it again last night, and a flood of memories came rushing back."

"Good or bad?" she asked, adjusting her chair so she has a more direct view of me on the couch.

"Both," I replied. "I didn't realize how much I related to Noelle, the main character. In the movie, she has an epiphany and begins to use her beauty to control men; it's where she got her power."

I paused and thought about what I just said, then asked, "Do you think that's a 'why' or 'where' I changed and followed this path?"

"I think you blame yourself too much for what happened to you as a child," she answered.

"The part of the film that haunts me is when her father traded her to an older, overweight businessman. He capitalized on her beauty and sold her as a mistress; it reminded me of a story I had long ago put to bed." I looked at her, then added, "Pun intended."

I uncrossed and then recrossed my legs. My legs that have gotten me in more trouble than any other part of my body. Well, unless you count my breasts. My legs are long, fit, and shapely, and they flow down to my arched feet, which look like they are made for high heels. My sister Kim calls them "Barbie feet." If the shoe fits . . . I was wearing Manolo Blahniks that day, the perfect pair of classic black pumps, and a simple sheath of black silk.

"Tell me about the story you mentioned. The one you 'put to bed.'"

"I was in college, I think it was my sophomore year after Brumby and after my year of Baptist repentance for my 'crime.' It was before I met the man who would end up being my first husband. Only God knows why I was home that particular weekend. It was springtime, so maybe it was spring break. The reason I know it was springtime was because I was dressed in a hot pink linen sundress that was cut just a little too low for someone with my sized breasts."

"Do you always remember what you were wearing?" Her question was pronounced and targeted.

"I was into fashion, always have been. I pretty much remember what I was wearing for most of the events in my life, especially when something significant takes place. I have one of those memories where I can close my eyes and find myself right back in the scene of it all; I remember what I wore, how I felt, the sounds, the smells, the tastes . . . Besides, being appropriately dressed for every occasion was as much a part of my childhood as learning to set a table or throw a proper dinner party. It was Mother's influence and her attempt to groom us to grow up to be the perfect wives."

"I didn't mean to sidetrack your thoughts," she apologized.

"Creative people are easily distracted and always welcome the distraction," I told her. "Anyway, I was home from college and my sister Jennifer (who was married and had been out of the house for a while) wanted me to go with her to meet her friends for drinks at a bar by the airport. Modine Gunch's, I think," I said as an afterthought.

"Jennifer, who, after years of self-medicating chose to deal drugs as her career path, came to the house with her best friends from high school, and we all headed to the bar. I was clueless as to why I'd been invited to join Jennifer on her 'girls' night out' but didn't question her. I found Jennifer to be one of the wildest, funniest people to party with; she was brilliantly wicked and always full of surprises." In my mind, I thought: *Plus, it was nice to be with my sister, since we had drifted apart, our circumstances having changed.*

"We arrived at the bar and grabbed a cocktail table. There was music playing, so we danced. The girls ordered a bottle of nice champagne (Dom Pérignon) and explained to me that our entire evening was being taken care of by a friend of theirs who might be joining us later. I didn't ask any questions; I just enjoyed the champagne as any college student would, and of course, spending time with my sister."

"Did you think it was slightly odd that you were all drinking one of the most expensive champagnes available?" Dr. H asked.

"No," I explained. "I was accustomed to men trying to impress me by sending Dom over to the table. Funny thing is, I really don't care for Dom. I much prefer Laurent-Perrier." This was all beside the point.

"After an hour or so, this older gentleman, probably early forties, showed up. He was overweight and balding but wearing an expensive suit. He sat at the high-top table with us but had nothing to contribute. Jennifer and her girlfriends kept pushing me to dance with him, which I found strange. I wasn't interested in him *at all*."

"How many of you were there?" she asked. *That's an unusual question*, I thought. "Counting me, there were five girls. All my sister's friends. I have no idea how they knew this man or where they met him, but I felt as if they were trying to push him on me. I quickly became uncomfortable and excused myself to go to the bathroom. While I was washing my hands, two of Jennifer's friends came into the bathroom lobby. They started talking about how rich this guy was, telling me what kind of car he drove, and that he would hook them up with drugs; all I had to do was 'be nice to him.' Perhaps I had a puzzled look on my face, because then they told me he would pay them $1,500—I would get $1,000 and they would get $500—if I would just dance with him."

Suddenly, tears welled up in my eyes. I could feel them, even though I mentally tried to stop their flow. *What was it about sterile bathrooms and realizations? What was it about me?*

"So, your sister and her friends basically pimped you out?" Dr. H asked, as she looked at me with disbelief and handed me a tissue.

"Yes," I answered, taking the tissue from her hand. "I couldn't believe it. I was so shocked. I pulled away from their embrace, left the bathroom, grabbed my jacket from the chair, and found a cab home. I didn't speak to any of them, especially my sister. I was hurt and humiliated that they would lure me under false pretenses and then use me to secure money and drugs. And 'all I had to do' was dance with him a few times. Who does that to their own sister?" I stopped talking for a moment to catch my breath and wipe the tears now streaming down my face.

"You know better than most how troubled drug addicts are. They don't care what they have to do to get money for drugs, or who they end up hurting in the process." Dr. H was trying to calm me.

"Yes, but how did they come up with this guy? Where'd they find him? And did they honestly think that all he really wanted was to dance with me? How did they sell me to him?"

"You never asked Jennifer?"

"No. We never spoke about it. Never once did it ever come up. Baptist housekeeping at its best."

"I'm beginning to see your pattern of sweeping things under the rug. There seems to be a lot underneath," Dr. H said with a strong tone of empathy in her voice.

I nodded *yes*, but my mind drifted off to *The Other Side of Midnight* and the pained look on Noelle's face; the emptiness in her eyes when the forty-something, overweight bald man who her father sold her to climbed on top of her and started to fuck her.

I saw it in her eyes . . . the determination of her spirit, however broken; it was then that she made her decision to leave. And it would be this same spirit that would propel me to leave my marriages when my heart said "no more" and the light from my eyes had been extinguished.

Chapter 12
Leopard is a Neutral

She had lit my favorite candle, and the scent of the sea was wafting in the air, making me smile. It wasn't long before that very few things made me smile, but I was finding it in myself to feel again. It was mid-March; we had been meeting for almost a year. I was a stronger person, which was perhaps the reason I was wearing my very fitted Moschino leopard print dress and high-heeled black stiletto sandals that might as well say, "Come fuck me." She noticed them immediately.

"You seem amused today," Dr. H observed as I walked into her office.

"I am happy," I responded. "I am starting to feel like my old self again."

"Leopard during the day?" she smiled, knowing that I have taught her a lot about fashion over the many sessions we've had.

"You know what I always say," I smiled back. "Leopard is a neutral."

She laughed and motioned for me to sit down on the familiar couch. She offered me a LaCroix. We had become very close, and I felt that we were getting to a point where my therapy has taken a turn . . . and so have I.

"What are you sharing today?" she asked.

"I have been thinking about my first husband a lot lately," I responded. "I guess that's why I wore leopard today. You know what they say about leopards . . . they never change their spots."

"The one who was so jealous?"

"No," I replied and then explained. "Mike was the jealous one, but he was my second husband."

"You've been married three times?" she seems shocked. "Have you mentioned this before?"

"I thought I did; it's hard to keep track sometimes." I smiled. "It was my starter marriage; my college sweetheart," I responded, knowing it was strange I hadn't brought him up in almost a year of therapy. "Let's call him BD. We were young, and he asked me to marry him. I was a senior in college, and I said yes."

"Why?" she asked, still a little flabbergasted.

"Because all my life that's all I knew. My mother was good at preparing my sisters and me to be the best wives possible; it was Daddy who insisted we get an education so we wouldn't have to depend on a man. Yet Mother was there the whole time, grooming us to be the perfect spouses: always dress for your husband, have his favorite drink in hand and greet him at the door when he comes home from work. Mother waited on my father hand and foot, and she was always perfectly coiffed. We learned to prepare the meals and to enjoy cleaning up afterwards. She made sure Daddy didn't have to lift a finger. He was the provider and we catered to him.

"So when it came time for me to graduate, I looked for a career, but I was also engaged."

"What happened?" she asked.

"Reality happened," I replied. "I didn't know it, but BD was a pathological liar. He told everyone what they wanted to hear."

"Sounds like someone else we've talked about," and she made a note.

"I know. I keep making the same mistakes." I can acknowledge this now.

"Give me an example of one of his lies." She was curious.

"Wow," I mused. "So many to choose from."

"Perhaps the biggest—or one of the biggest—and best, was the one regarding the wedding." I stopped to see if she was going to ask another question, but she didn't say anything. So I continued.

"My first job after graduating from UGA with a journalism degree was as a reporter for one of the local neighborhood papers. It paid next to nothing, but I loved it! BD had asked me to marry him just after New Year's Eve, while I was visiting him in Milwaukee."

"He wasn't from Atlanta?" She was puzzled.

"No, I met him during spring break my junior year of college. But that is an entirely different story."

"Let's stick with the wedding story for now."

"I was at his parents' home in Greenfield, Wisconsin, which is just shy of Milwaukee. He was attending MSOE, Milwaukee School of Engineering, having left the University of Wisconsin in Madison, where he attended the spring we met. But I digress, because that is yet another story. Sorry.

"I said yes when he proposed, and when I went home, I told my parents. I was getting ready to graduate early from college in March, having completed all of my credits. In hindsight, it was the best thing since my favorite grandmother had been diagnosed with lung cancer the prior year, and I ended up spending most of my time with her from March until the graduation ceremony in June. I loved listening to her stories from when she grew up. She was a natural storyteller. I actually wrote my first novel based on a story she told me. It was about her childhood nanny."

"You are getting off subject again," she said, reining me back in to focus on my first wedding.

"I tend to do that when I'm about to reveal an unpleasant part of my past," I remarked. I had become much more self-aware after a year in therapy, and isn't procrastination a sign of childhood trauma?

She nodded and waited for me.

"Anyway, I start . . . or rather, my mother starts to plan the wedding. I am working long hours as a reporter—going into the small office by day and covering government meetings and chamber events during the evenings. Then, I would go into the office and file my stories, only to repeat it the next day. At the same time, I am picking out a bridal gown and emerald-green taffeta bridesmaids' dresses for a New Year's Eve wedding.

"After careful consideration, I decided on twelve bridesmaids."

"Twelve?" She raised her eyebrows in true astonishment.

"Yes," I answered. "Twelve. Looking back now, it seems quite excessive. But what you have to remember is I have a lot of friends and family, and we couldn't leave anyone out. Besides, it was my mother's wedding as much as it was mine."

"I see," she made a note in her book again.

"BD had four sisters, and I asked two of them to be in the wedding, along with both his brothers. When it came time to order the dresses, I kept pressing him for his sister's sizes. He kept delaying getting them to me. Finally, he sent them along with his list of wedding guests. This would have been around July or August for the December wedding. My mother kept pushing and pushing for me to get the information from him.

"Everything was coming along well. We ordered the invitations, and they came in and Mother immediately began to address the envelopes. We have BD's wedding list and his sisters' sizes. Now comes time to reserve the hotel for the rehearsal dinner. Since his family is out of state, I offer to make the arrangements. I send him the menus and room charges along with a contract for his parents to complete. It is mid-October, and we are six weeks out from the wedding."

"I am afraid I see where this is heading," she said.

I laughed an uncomfortable laugh and wondered if she really knew. I hadn't thought about this in years . . . damn iceberg.

"I am at work, and I made a comment to one of the advertising sales reps that I haven't heard back from BD's mother about the rehearsal dinner. She tells me that I should call his mother directly and talk to her myself. She then offers me a calling card so I can use the office phone. Remember this is 1983, way before cell phones. And long-distance phone communication was nowhere near the level it is today," I said, stating the obvious.

"So I rang up his mother and asked her if she had any questions about the menu because I needed to let the hotel know about the rooms and that the bridesmaids' dresses should be in any day." I paused for a minute, remembering my future mother-in-law's voice on the other end of the line.

"And?" Dr. H looked at me with sadness in her eyes—a look I had seen way too often.

"She has no idea what I am talking about. I try to hold back my tears, but they immediately start to flow. She calms me down and tells me everything is going to be fine. That she would get with BD and then get back to me. I hung up the phone. Everyone in the office knows what's happening now because they overhear me. I am humiliated."

"His family didn't know about the wedding?"

"Had no clue. BD hadn't given them the package I sent back with him in July. Turns out he just went into his sisters' closets and looked inside their clothes for sizes."

"So the wedding went ahead as planned?" she said with complete surprise in her voice.

"That's the best part," I said. "My editor told me to go home and compose myself. I leave the office and drive home in tears. I walk in the door sobbing and tell my mother I want to call off the wedding."

"And her response was?"

"She told me it was too late. She had just finished sending out the invitations. The bridal showers had all been planned, and gifts had begun to come in. She said if I wanted to contact all three hundred people we had invited and tell them it was off, I could. 'But how would that look?'"

"You went through with a wedding you knew was doomed." It was a statement, not a question.

"I cried before I went down the aisle," I told her. "My sister Jennifer told me I didn't have to go through with it. Tom, my sorority sister Nancy's husband, whom I had been in college with, too, told me he would pull up his truck and I could run out the side door. All options I should have taken." I am sad as I remember how I felt on my wedding day. "We fought on the way to the hotel after the reception. I knew it was over before it even began. The only thing I didn't know was how long it would last."

"How long did it last?"

"Technically, three years. But in reality, it was only a good six months—or six hours depending on which breakup counts. I will say that when I moved to Milwaukee, I was able to land a great job as a special events coordinator for Gimbels, Midwest. It was in the Gimbels job that I honed my promotional and special event skills. I never regretted that aspect of the relationship."

"You moved to Milwaukee?"

"Yes. He still had a couple of semesters left before he graduated, or so I thought. That's another pathological lie story, and I am tired and don't want to go there now."

"And our time is up anyway; we will have to address this next time."

"And my *9 1/2 Weeks* awakening," I said, realizing we got sidetracked again.

"Yes, she smiled. "What is that again?"

"A movie I saw after I divorced BD . . . right around the time I met the girls' dad. I guess I had been intrigued by that world ever since I saw the movie with Kim Basinger and Mickey Rourke."

"What world are you speaking about? "

"As a young girl, I had read about sex in books like *Once Is Not Enough* by Jacqueline Susann. And then there was the movie *The Other Side of Midnight*

I told you about early on that really made an impression on me at the ripe age of 17. But it wasn't until I saw *9 1/2 Weeks* that I really started to explore my own sexuality."

"Go on," she said.

"I 'got it' by the time I was 25 years old. After the movie, I began to wear stockings and garter belts and sexy underwear. It just turned me on and made me want to dress like that . . . you know, secretly, for myself. I dressed like that for me. Black skirt and white blouse—very sedate on the outside. But underneath . . . I felt sexy. It just all came together for me after that movie."

I left her office with a little less spring in my step than when I arrived. I knew the point of therapy is to talk about these hard, embarrassing moments and try to make sense out of them. I was beginning to think that maybe Mother's way is the best, just a total blockage of uncomfortable times. Hiding them away in the back of the closet like an unused gift.

I was cold and frigid inside from diving too far deep into those old icy waters, and my leopard print dress and patent leather stiletto sandals suddenly seemed inappropriate and way out of season.

Chapter 13
How I Met Your Father

"You know you're not my first," I began. "Therapist, that is." I clarified my statement as I fumbled through my black Prada purse with large black emerald-cut stones fastened to the front. It's one of my favorite bags that I kept. Maybe a reminder that I went from Prada to nada. . .

"I think you mentioned it to me when we first started our sessions," the doctor responded. "Why do you find that necessary to bring up today?"

"I don't know why I find any of this necessary to bring up. It's been shuttered for so long; some of the memories are only found in my own poetry but also in lines written by others." I pulled out some papers from my bag. "I found this one verse and it reminded me of my first therapist, the one who told me I had a classic case of Cinderella syndrome. I laughed and told her I could have guessed that without paying her for the diagnosis. Not only do I have a shoe fetish, but I think I was always waiting for someone to rescue me."

"Why do you think that's true?" Dr. H asked.

"I think it is part of who I am and always will be. Mother was very insecure and always said she married Daddy because he gave her security. But this poem made me realize that I can make bold decisions, like the one I made when I divorced the girls' father. No one understood or supported my decision, except my sisters."

"You haven't spoken too much about the girls' dad. I assumed he was not an issue."

"You don't speak of gods and monsters."

I handed her the paper with the following words written:

"If you love something, set it free. If it comes back, it was, and always will be yours. If it never returns, it was never yours to begin with."

—Fritz Perls

"But this is the one that reminds me of Mike." I gave her the second sheet.

"If you love something/Set it free/If it loves you/It will come back to you/ If it doesn't—hunt it down and kill it."

—Harry Crews

"I remember these quotes from when I began dating the girls' father," I said as I handed Dr. H the slip of my engraved Tiffany & Co. stationery. "The first one Mike actually told me about. But then I found this other one years later, and I think it reflects his true intentions."

She took both pieces of paper in her hands and read them. She was wearing a black pantsuit with a simple white blouse, and today she reminded me of my third-grade teacher, Miss Moss. Maybe it's the dirty brown bobbed wig she was wearing or the way she held the notes, one in each hand. But, in my mind, I was 8 years old, transferred back to Tara Elementary School as I looked at my doctor. She was very pretty but composed in a way so as not to attract attention. Maybe she had as many secrets to hide as I?

She interrupted my thoughts.

"Tell me about the first time you heard this quote and why it reminds you of the girls' father," she began. "Then I want to hear about how you think the second quote reflects the true relationship you developed with him."

I adjusted my very expensive cream knit St. John dress with the emerald cut gold buttons and began.

"I was only 26 when I met Mike. He was ten years older than me, married with two children, and he was also my boss. I was working for the county commissioners' office as the public information officer. I was the youngest PIO in the country," I added this last sentence proudly and smiled.

"And you know this fact, because?" she asked.

"I was invited to speak in Baltimore at a convention, and that's when I found out what a novelty I was. I was not only the youngest PIO, but also one of the few females. Most public information officers were middle-aged white guys who used to write for their local papers until the political powers scooped them up."

"Anyway, I was offered the position, not only because I was qualified, which I was because of my degree in journalism, but also because the commission chairman happened to be my parents' friend and my father's golfing buddy."

"Did you feel qualified to be in such a position?" She made notations in her book and did not look up at me.

"I think it's like any job. If you've never done it before, there is a bit of trepidation when you walk into a new position. But after a while you begin to learn not only the job, but what is expected of you. I find kindness goes a long way in any situation. Be kind to people, and they will show you the way."

"That's a great attitude to have and I am sure one that has served you well over the years." She looked up over her glasses and smiled. She was even prettier when she smiled.

"Do you know what the difference is between sexual harassment and flirt-ing in the workplace?" I asked, looking right at her without blinking to let her know it was a serious question.

"No," she answered.

"Well, if you are attracted to the person, it's considered flirting. If you are put off by the person, it's sexual harassment. That's at least how I see it. It's my own private joke."

She didn't laugh.

"It's a Yes versus a No. Anyway," I continued, breaking the awkwardness. "VF, the commission chairman, who was the most powerful government offi-cial in the county, started off initially by requiring that I accompany him to meetings and events that the other PIO never had to attend. I didn't realize it until his private secretary began to question me about my role. I was young and afraid to say anything; it became increasingly uncomfortable.

"I shudder when I think of the scared little girl I became when I was just starting out; thinking of how proud I was to be the youngest PIO in the coun-try, yet I was dodging my boss's boss at every turn. I remember this one inci-dent when the harassment really began to escalate. It was winter because I was wearing a pink plaid wool coat dress and flesh-colored fishnet stockings.

"Flesh-colored fishnets?" She had a look of concern in her eyes, and I knew immediately what she was inferring.

"Anyway, this particular evening we were leaving an event—he insisted that I ride with him instead of meeting him at the venue, and instead of tak-ing me back to my car, he pulled into a local motel. I was shocked and scared and didn't know what to do. He looked at me and said, 'Is this OK?' I guess he had gotten the room earlier that day, or perhaps he had the room on a regular basis, because he pulled right up to the door, key in hand and told me to 'come on.' So I got out of the car and followed him. Remember: I was 25 years old, newly divorced, and protectively naive." I thought back to that moment, and

I could still feel the strangeness of it all. It was if I was watching someone else, someone who was numb and scared and afraid to say no.

"He takes me in the room, and again, he doesn't say anything, just begins to awkwardly make his move by sitting on the bed and motioning me to sit next to him. Then he begins to kiss me, and I am repulsed. All I can think of is that he is old and my father's friend, that he's my boss and that he wears a toupee." I can still feel his breath on me as I recall that evening, and once again I feel the numbness, the awkwardness of being in a situation in which you have no control. I am sick that I didn't ask him to stop.

"Did he rape you?" she asked.

"No," I said. "But not for the reason you think. I don't believe he was going to rape me. I think he was just trying to see how far he could get. I am embarrassed that he got me to the room, but then I felt as if I had no voice. Funny thing is that I was paralyzed at the moment he began to kiss me. It's when he started to touch me and make his way down to my legs that I remembered I had a hole in one of my stockings from bumping into a filing cabinet earlier that day. I was going to go home and change, but he insisted that I ride with him to the event . . . so I never did. When I realized that I still had on the pantyhose with the hole—and I know this sounds strange—it gave me the courage to ask him to stop." *Isn't it odd that the imperfection of my undergarment was the reason I asked him to stop?*

"I asked him to stop and take me back to my car, and he did. Funny, but I do not remember much more about that night. Just that I was repulsed and literally silenced by my fear, frozen by my inability to make it stop. I know I did not want to go with him into that motel room, yet I did. I was so afraid of him that I relinquished all my power of just saying no.

"After that incident, he started to call me late at night and drop by my apartment unannounced. That is when I got the courage to go talk to my immediate boss, who happened to be Mike, and told him everything that was going on. Mike told me he would take care of it, and in his own way he did."

"How did he handle the situation?" she asked.

"By accompanying me to every event I was involved in or that VF, the commission chairman, made me attend. It was a crazy sideshow now that I look back on it. These two grown men in stare-downs with each other over me. They did everything but pull their penises out for comparison. It was comical really." I sat in silence as I remembered something my mother said when I told her about VF's advances. She asked me not to tell my father; they were golfing buddies, and he didn't need to know. I picked up my thoughts and continued.

"So, Mike and I got together. Seems he fell in love with me. I resisted at first since he was married with two kids, but he showered me with gifts and trips . . . you know the story." I thought to myself that the problem with someone sweeping you off your feet is that, eventually, you have to be placed back down on the ground. It's the landing that always hurts more than the high that walking on air ever provides.

She stopped writing in her book and nodded. "Yes, I've heard this kind of story before. How does this relate to the quotes?"

"I'm getting there," I answered. "The more Mike pursued me, the more I began to pull back. He was showering me with expensive gifts and jewelry, as well as numerous shopping trips to Lenox Square to buy something for me to wear on our dates. But he was smothering me at the same time. Then one day, he told me he saw a bumper sticker with the saying: 'If you love something, set it free,' so he did. He eased up on the pursuit, and I eventually came around."

"How long did you see him before you were married?" she asked.

"I went to him in January about the harassment, which began just after I had gotten my divorce; I started seeing him in March and broke it off in April. He took me to St. Thomas for a week in May to celebrate my birthday, and when we returned he moved out of the house he shared with his wife and kids, and we moved into a condo together. I quit my job and traveled with him to Vegas, Hilton Head, and other places for him to golf and gamble. I remember he gave me money to shop for something to wear to Vegas, and then while we were in Vegas I shopped for more clothes. I shopped and drank champagne; he gambled and drank whiskey. We were the perfect pair; he knew how to make money, and I knew how to spend it. He got divorced that summer, we got engaged in September and married in November."

"All in the same year?" she had that look on her face that told me she didn't approve.

"Yes, all in the same year. It was a whirlwind."

"And when did this second quote you gave me come to define your relationship?"

"Let me see," I said, pausing to do the math in my head. "We bought a new house in the quaint town of Fayetteville and moved in right before we got married. That was in November 1987. I spent the entire year of '88 decorating the house with a well-known designer in town. I picked out all the wallcoverings and fabric and had custom drapes and bedding made. I have no idea what I spent. I just made my choices, and he paid for them." I recognized the irony in my last statement because, in the end, it was I who paid the highest price.

"Decorating, shopping, and traveling—that's how I spent my first year of marriage. We would have dinner parties and attend a lot of exclusive events. I was always on his arm for something or other."

"So you were his trophy?"

"Yes. I guess I had already achieved trophy wife status at the ripe old age of 27. That is if you can be considered a trophy wife in Fayetteville, Georgia." I laughed.

"When did it start to go wrong?" She looked up with her kind eyes and waited for the answer.

"When I got my dream job."

"Did you want to go back to work?"

"I wasn't looking to go back to work, but this incredible opportunity came up. I was not going to let it pass me by."

"Which was?"

"I pitched the team at Turner Broadcasting on the fiftieth anniversary of *Gone with the Wind,* and they hired me to produce the event. It was my dream job; you know, the one with the company you have always wanted to work for with the project that comes around every fifty years about a movie that is still a classic today? That's when his jealousy came out."

"You never saw it before you went back to work?"

"No. He always had control of where I was and what I did before that. But when I went back to work, he lost control. His insecurities were revealed. Daily."

I tried to put the image of me as a scared little girl out of my mind, but I couldn't. I could still feel his anger as it emanated out of his every pore. The silent treatment that left me alone and bruised on the inside. Constantly turning events over and over in my mind; the second-guessing of trying to figure out just what I did wrong. His jealousy was so strong that I can still feel it today, even though I am many years removed from him. I can still feel the emptiness of my soul, the sorrow and bewilderment of not knowing what I had done wrong. I think of the different times when I saw the raw open vastness of rage coming from his eyes.

Every once in a while, in the quiet hours when I allow my mind to wander, I am reminded of those days when I felt so alone, when he was the hunter, and I was his prey.

Chapter 14
I Don't Give a Damn, Frankly

"I picture myself on that day in the fall of 1989. I was seven months pregnant with Lydia and working my dream job for Turner Entertainment as the coordinating director of the fiftieth anniversary of the iconic movie *Gone with the Wind*. It should have been a momentous year for me; having my first child and producing the ten-day event for Turner, but it was filled with moments of fear, torture, and tears."

"This sounds like a very traumatic event for you," Dr. H observed. "Have you spoken about it often?"

"No, no one ever knew just how much hell I went through in 1989—not my family, or my immediate boss, or coworkers, or friends. I pretended that everything was OK, just the usual stress of creating a life and a major event for a Fortune-whatever company at the same time. But the way I was treated by my husband, Mike, as I tried to hold everything together?" I shook my head at the memory. "I will never forgive him.

"How can you profess to love somebody and then be so intentionally cruel?" I asked. "I found out much later that it was because he was 'pathologically jealous' where I was concerned. I am sure you are aware of the term?"

"Yes, very aware," she said. "In fact, I was reading up on it this morning." She pointed to a medical journal. "It's also known as morbid jealousy or 'Othello syndrome.'"

"'O beware, my lord, of jealousy! It is the green-eyed monster which doth mock the meat it feeds on,'" I quoted the famous line from Shakespeare's *Othello*. "That pretty much sums up my marriage to Mike. He was a green-eyed monster, so afraid that I was going to cheat on him that he tortured me emotionally on a daily basis—and just one year into our marriage. One particular incident, however, during that year of my greatest professional triumph, made me realize that one day I would leave him. I didn't know when or how or what I was going to do, but I knew that my love for him was gone—forever altered, broken—like me."

"You have to stop looking at yourself as being broken," she warned. "The fact that you have endured this pain your entire life and risen above it speaks volumes about your character and your self-worth."

"It speaks volumes about my brokenness," I corrected her as she gave me the look of "you know better." Then I started to tell the story of the beginning of the end.

"I was working in downtown Atlanta at the CNN Center, where Turner Broadcasting's offices were then located. For seven months I had been getting up at four a.m. to do my research and work on my special event planning for the fiftieth anniversary celebration. I would leave for the office after Mike left the house at nine a.m. so I could be home early in the afternoon before he came home.

"That was one of the requirements he placed on me to be able to do this project: I had to be home when he got home. Normally, that would be between five and six p.m. But as time got closer to the December event, he started coming home earlier and earlier—so I would have to leave the office earlier and earlier.

"One day in September, right after his birthday, he was furious at me. We had been to a dinner party with some of his colleagues, and one of the men mentioned how great it was that I was the person responsible for planning this huge event for Turner. I'm not sure why, but Mike was so mad by the time we left the party, he wasn't speaking to me. He actually got out of the car about a mile or so before we arrived home and walked the rest of the way.

"I circled back around a couple of times and tried to make him get back in the car, but he refused. So I went home and went to bed."

I took a sip of my LaCroix and traced the houndstooth pattern of my skirt with my finger, a nervous habit that had become a ritual, before I continued.

"I left for the office the next morning without him acknowledging me. I was so frightened and anxious and pregnant. I didn't know what else to do. When he got like this, he would 'punish' me by not speaking to me, so I learned to keep doing what I needed to do until he came around. But this time was different.

"I was at the office trying to arrange a cast reunion party and dealing with Olivia de Havilland's people in Paris, without much success. I was anxiety laden when I got the call from my assistant, Nettie: 'Your husband's on line one.' I was so sick to my stomach not knowing what to expect, but I knew I had to take the call.

"'I'm getting ready to leave the office; you better be home by the time I get there,' he basically commanded, and then he hung up."

Dr. H noticed that I was agitated and almost hyperventilating as I mentally put myself back in the moment. She asked if I wanted to take a break. I said no.

"It was two o'clock in the afternoon, and I had so much work I needed to do. But I also knew I had better leave the office and head home, knowing that his office was fifteen minutes away; mine was forty minutes. I knew I would never make it home before he arrived, yet I packed up my work and made my way from my tenth floor office, down the elevator, and across the street to the CNN employee parking deck.

"I was holding the bottom of my seven-months pregnant belly, running as fast as I could to my car, crying. I don't remember exactly what my thoughts were; I only know I was terrified of what I would find when I got home. It put a whole new meaning on the book *What to Expect When You're Expecting*." I let out a nervous laugh.

"And what did you find when you got home?" she asked as she handed me a tissue.

"His car was in the driveway; parked in the guest drive in the front of the house so I would see it as soon as I made the turn. I parked in front of the garage and made my way to the front of the house. The doors were locked, so I fumbled for my key in my purse. I walked in and he immediately started talking to me as if I were a child who had missed her curfew. He was standing over me in the kitchen, going on and on about how I am his wife and when he is home I need to be home too. He reminded me that it was our agreement if he *allowed* me to do this contract project, that it could *not* interfere with his wants and needs.

"I remember being so very frightened and cowering in the corner of the kitchen, on the floor crying. I don't know how long I was there, but I did make it to the phone tethered to the kitchen wall, and I called my father to come and pick me up. That was the wrong thing to do . . .

"Mike was furious when my parents showed up, but he had calmed down and convinced them that I was OK. He never hit me or raised his hand to me, but I was beaten down just the same. My parents ended up leaving our house, leaving me there.

"I can't remember how the night ended after they left, or much afterwards. I know that it was swept under the rug and not mentioned again. I knew better than to point out his cruel behavior.

"I went on to give birth to my first daughter on December fifth, five days before the beginning of the ten-day *Gone with the Wind* Fiftieth Anniversary Celebration for the city of Atlanta. I wasn't due until later in the month, but the stress from trying to pull off a major event and being pregnant while in an abusive marriage was too much for even me to handle."

"I think we should stop here now." Dr. H got up from her chair. "You look exhausted."

I told her I was and then I left her office with my head held high and my mind racing. I was mentally exhausted, and the rush of the anxiety and the feeling of running toward doom hit me as I walked out the door. Once again, I was that little girl, in a wet swimsuit, being chased and crying out as I ran as fast as my suntanned legs could carry me into the arms of my father.

Chapter 15
Lydia Grace

I was empowered from my last appointment and what I revealed—a cleansing of feelings and truths, secrets only known to myself, until now. Was I ready to begin again? I thought so. Insanity seems to bring out the reality of it all. Yet somehow, I welcomed this fall from grace, this season of my life. How apropos that I love this time of year, for it reminds me of new beginnings, even though the falling leaves seem to speak otherwise. I reached down and traced the hemline of my outfit with my newly manicured nails. I was wearing the coat to an old St. John knit suit I bought in New York, one that needs to be retired but still makes me feel happy when I put it on. That's what Mother always told me: if you have something that makes you feel good, do not get rid of it. That's funny coming from a woman who threw out last-year's fashion every season, including her bespoke yellow chiffon wedding dress and all of her custom Delta uniforms. This St. John knit is a simple long black jacket with signature buttons. I paired it with skinny jeans. It is timeless and worked well with my new Miu Miu black suede pumps with six-inch heels I had just picked up from Jeffrey. What is it they say? "If I'm going to take the high road, I'm going to need new shoes." Yes, I felt good about my choices that day, sanity aside.

"I remembered what I was going to say next," I told Dr. H as our next session began.

It had only been two days since we last talked, yet it seemed like two weeks. I had asked to come see her again; I don't know why I felt it was so urgent, but she worked me in.

"I'm glad we were able to get you on the schedule," she said. "I was worried when I saw your name."

"That's funny that you say that," I responded. "It's how my sister, my cousin, and my best friend react whenever I call them late at night. They always take my call." I laughed, knowing that my sister Kim, cousin Josh, and BFF Kelly have each answered the phone at two in the morning with the same question: "Are you OK?"

"When someone you love feels desperate to end their life, it's an urgent matter." She sounded very doctorly. "I know your sister, cousin, and friend must love you and support you enough to take your call."

"They do, and I have only shared with them my story because I feel so close to them, and I wanted to let them in."

"Again, that's a positive sign."

"I know. It's when I don't get in touch or don't call or don't reach out, that's when you know I am in trouble."

"Speaking of that," she asked, "what brings you back this week?"

"I wanted to finish my story." I said. "I think it's important for you to know the rest. I know I left off with the birth of my first daughter, Lydia."

"That's a beautiful name," she said.

"Thank you. Her full name is Lydia Grace. She is named after my favorite aunt, Lydia Gail, and my mother, Grace. So it's a very special name to me. Anyway, I wanted to tell you this because I remember it so well.

"I had a verbal fight with the Fox Theatre guy about who was going to get the sponsorship money I had raised for the event. Just one of the many 'perks' of producing a major event while pregnant. I knew with all the stress I'd been under, that I would be giving birth early. And sure enough, at midnight, I started having contractions. So Mike and I called the doctor, and we headed to Piedmont Hospital in Atlanta.

"I was in labor all night, and then at nine in the morning the nurse comes in and tells me it's time for my epidural booster, but she thinks I will deliver soon so she talks me into not getting the medicine. Well by eleven-thirty a.m., when I still haven't delivered her, that damn epidural has worn off and the doctor warns me that he will have to vacuum her out or I will have to have a C-section."

"Vacuum?"

"Yes, they actually put a suction machine on the head and pull the baby out of the birth canal. She was born via suction at eleven fifty-five; almost three hours after my epidural wore off. I was exhausted and tired and hungry, and I remember, when they placed her in my arms, I felt empty."

"Why do you think that is?"

"I have thought about it often. The childbirth class nurse told us, 'The minute they place the baby in your arms, you will feel this immediate sense of joy,' and that didn't happen. I was holding this tiny creature thinking to myself, 'It's not happening, no bonding going on here.'

"Anyway, I had been at the hospital since midnight and hadn't eaten anything since dinner the night before. By the time I got to my room, I had missed lunch. And I wanted my mother."

"She wasn't there for the birth?"

"No," I said, "Mike didn't call her. And it was before cell phones. He called her that morning to tell her I was at the hospital, or I called her at midnight to tell her I was going to Piedmont. I can't remember which. All I know is, he didn't let her know that Lydia had been born. She and Daddy just showed up at the hospital around two in the afternoon along with my sisters. They hadn't heard from him, so Mother and crew came anyway."

"Why didn't he call them?"

"I've often thought about that too. I think it was a control thing. He didn't want to share me. Who knows what it was. It was Mike."

"I didn't mean to interrupt your thoughts," she said, but I welcomed the interruption. I was trying to go back and remember that day, those feelings, the tired and the hurt and the hunger.

"I remember my sister Jennifer saying: 'I'm glad it's not a Tad.'" I laughed with tears in my eyes.

"What is a Tad?"

"That was what we were going to call the baby if it was a boy, name him after Mike and call him Tad. So she was glad I had had a girl."

I took a sip of my water, a new grapefruit sparkling drink. Five calories. I thought of how hard it is to get baby weight off; men are so clueless. And simple, I thought. *Men are simple; it's we who complicate them. Giving them thoughts and feelings when all they really have with any sort of feeling is a dick. Feed, suck, and fuck them, and they are happy creatures. Primal needs.*

"I miss my sister." I started to cry.

"I know you do," she answered, handed me a box of tissues, and waited for me to compose myself.

"They all came to see the baby—my friends, family. Flowers were sent, champagne was smuggled in." I laughed, "I didn't know you couldn't have alcohol in a hospital.

"By eight p.m. that evening, Mike had sent everyone away. Even Mother. He told her he would be staying with me. She had been there since the early afternoon, long before I was put into a room, waiting on me. And now, he sent her and Daddy home. He told them he would be there with me."

"I'm sensing this is the part you want to share with me," she stated.

"Yes," I said. "This is the part that always reminds me why I hate him. Not the nights he wouldn't speak to me, or the days he sat in silence in the living room. Not the cold shoulder or the 'it's just not rights'; not the cowering in the corner of the kitchen or the awkwardness of when my parents knew he didn't want them around. No, not all the other things that happened before or after Lydia was born. But it was this *one* moment when I knew that I was going to one day leave."

"What happened?" She brought me back to the subject matter.

"It'd been twenty-four hours since I'd eaten. I'd been through twelve hours of labor, natural childbirth with the help of a Hoover, the nervousness of having a human being that is totally dependent on me, the sending away of my mother when I wanted her and needed her. Then he closes the door to the room, looks at the crib next to the bed, and after about thirty minutes says he was heading home."

"So he left you there?"

"Yes, he left me. Alone. With a baby. Well, actually, they had come and gotten Lydia. I was planning to nurse her, and they came and got her about nine p.m. The nurse said they would take her to the nursery, and they would bring her back when she wanted me. I asked the nurse if I could get something to eat, but the meal service was long over and the cafeteria was closed."

"Wait," she interrupted. "You still hadn't eaten?"

"No," I said. I had so many visitors and Mike left to go get something to eat when my parents were there, but he failed to bring me something. Mother later told me that she and Daddy left so Mike and I could have some time alone; plus they got the feeling he didn't want them there. She had no idea that he didn't bring me back something to eat or that thirty minutes after they left, he would be leaving too."

"Wow, OK. I see now." That was her comment.

"The nurse came in around ten p.m. with some Lance's peanut butter crackers from the vending machine and a Coke. She promised me that the menu I filled out would start the next morning, and she would make sure I would get breakfast before she left. And then she left me alone in my room with my crackers and Coke and TV. I tried to sleep and finally did around midnight.

"Then at two a.m., the door opened and the nurse came into the room pushing the little crib with Lydia. She said, 'Someone wants their mommy.' She handed her to me and then it happened."

"What was that?"

"The bond. I cradled her, and she was so small and beautiful and helpless. And she wanted me. I nursed her, and I was in love. She was all I needed, and I was all she knew. And there in the dark, alone in my room, with only my newborn daughter, I knew everything would be OK."

"And Mike?"

"I already knew that it was over. I didn't know when I would leave, but I decided that very night that one day, I would."

Chapter 16

Ring of Fire

Mother always told me that men were stupid. She said, "If they only knew how simple it was to please a woman." It was, after all, the little things that truly count: running a bath, wiping a tear, putting a god-damned dish in the dishwasher.

Yet she never asked for anything, which was her own fault. Instead, she channeled her feelings of neglect in a positive way, by showering us girls with attention, gifts, and songs.

"What are we talking about today?" Dr. H asked before I had the chance to take off my black and white houndstooth wool coat and get comfortable on the blue denim couch.

I reflected on the fact that, for most of my life, rarely had I ever worn jeans, yet I had spent the last few months on a denim couch revealing secrets I never thought I would share. Is that ironic? I couldn't decide.

"It's my girls' birthdays and I can't afford to get them much, and it makes me sad and disappointed that I am where I am in my life." I began.

"I know they don't ask for much, they never had to. I always made sure they got all the things they wanted, or what I thought they wanted. Barbie's Dream everything. They were always dressed well; I bought their wardrobe by 'seasons.' I had a craft closet instead of a pantry, and our kitchen table was just one of their many playgrounds. They had their own den with a TV and games and dress-up clothes and books. I was a good mother." I began to cry.

"What has brought up these feelings?" she asked as she handed me a tissue.

"Did I tell you I sold my engagement ring when I left Bill?"

"I think you might have mentioned it," she responded.

"It was my dream ring, like Barbie." I laughed a little. "It was a four-carat, cushion-cut diamond, surrounded by diamonds; five-carat total weight. It was a replica of a Tiffany & Co. vintage ring. It was worth about $45,000, and I got a whopping $21,000 for it when I sold it after I left. That sale enabled me to live, although frugally, as I tried to pay back my debts while I tried to find a job."

"Then it was a good investment," she said.

"It was my only remaining asset worth selling. So yes, it was a good investment. I saved my other engagement ring for Lydia. It was a dreadful marquis diamond, two carats, set in yellow gold.

"Remember the scene from *Sex and the City* when Carrie makes fun of the ring Aiden was going to propose with? It was *that* ring." I laughed out loud. "Turned out Miranda helped him pick it out, but no girl wants a marquis set in yellow gold. Hello, the 1970s called, and they want their ring back!" I felt shallow making this last statement, and the Carpenters' "We've Only Just Begun" started playing in my mind until the doctor brought me back.

"You're off track again," she gently said.

"No, it goes to what I'm about to say. The funny thing is, I still have the marquis ring; I've saved it for Lydia. And my original pavé diamond platinum band from Bill, I have for Caroline. They were genuine and given with the best intentions. It was the Tiffany-style ring that was given to me that didn't really mean anything, so I was able to let it go."

"Even though it was your idea of what a ring should be." Dr. H wasn't asking a question.

"Exactly. Even though it was the ring I chose and was more valuable in monetary terms; it was not sentimental." I reflected on a similar moment from my youth that made such a big impression on me and decided to share it with Dr. H.

"I am reminded of a time when my father presented my mother with a ring for their fifteenth anniversary. I say 'presented,' because that is exactly what he did. He called us all together, and he presented her the ring in front of us girls. It was a white gold ring with two rows of five diamonds each. I thought it was the most beautiful ring I had ever seen. I was ten." I paused and remembered the first piece of jewelry I received. I was in second grade, and it was a rhinestone bracelet from Jeril Bliss. His mother called mine, and I had to give it back. It seems it belonged in her jewelry box, not in mine.

"Anyway, several years later, I found the ring in Mother's jewelry box. It had been gutted; the ten diamonds scattered about in insignificant pieces, three necklaces for the granddaughters and a ring with the rest. I showed Mother the setting and asked her why she broke up the ring that Daddy presented to her so many years before. I have never forgotten her response. It still haunts me to this day.

"She told me that the ring I thought so beautiful meant nothing to her because, and I quote, 'It was given to me at the lowest point of my marriage.'"

"Wow," Dr. H was compelled to respond. "That speaks volumes."

"Yes, it does." I said, "I think of her words a lot lately. And I find myself taking inventory of my life in those terms. The jewelry I received and for what purposes. The ones I saved for the girls, and the ones that are meaningless. Those are the ones that are easy to let go."

I looked down at my bare hands, in need of a manicure, and thought about the significance of a ring and what it really means to belong to someone.

Chapter 17
Sweet Caroline

There are events in life you know you should avoid, but which you are obligated to attend. I had started to feel this way about my sessions with Dr. H. Or maybe, I had gotten to a point in the sessions where the dialogue I knew was coming was on a subject matter that I would prefer to keep to myself. At any rate, I think she knew this. So I was not surprised when she wanted to talk about my other daughter, Caroline. My precious Caroline, whom I tried to protect, at great lengths, and whom I failed miserably.

"You haven't spoken of Caroline," Dr. H began. "I'm curious. Why?"

"She and I have an interesting dynamic," I confessed as I pulled down my greige cable knit dress so it touched my matching suede over-the-knee Stuart Weitzman boots.

"In what way?" She wasn't dropping the subject.

"She loves me, and she hates me," I responded. "She's my best friend and my worst critic. "She loves me, and she hates me," I responded. "She's my best friend and my worst critic. What is it that Kris Kristofferson wrote, something about being a walking contradiction?"

"So she was a challenge?"

"She was a difficult child, but not in the terms you're probably thinking."

"How so?" she pressed.

"First of all, I was sick with her the entire nine months of my pregnancy." I shudder at the memory; her dad nicknamed me Ziploc because I had to carry one on my person at all times, just in case. So I did not have an easy time with her from the beginning."

"When you say sick?"

"It's like this . . . imagine the worst hangover you've ever had; then imagine waking up every day for nine months feeling that way. And I mean from the time you wake up until you go to bed. I would get sick from the moment I woke until I went to sleep. And I mean gut-wrenching sick. No relief, except when I was eating, which is why I gained so much weight with her and why the doctor put me on meds so I could at least stop throwing up. I was miserable. Unfortunately, come to find out, she was sick too."

"What do you mean by that?"

"By that, I mean it turns out she had a birth defect."

"That explains why you were sick the entire pregnancy." She was nodding.

"I guess, but I also have this guilt that I might have caused it." *This is why I don't like going here*, I thought.

"How could you have caused it?"

"Because I was so sick, my doctor had me take medicine to ease my morning sickness, which is really a misnomer since I had all-day, every-God-damned-day sickness."

"What did he prescribe?"

"Well, that should have been my first clue. He said the medicine he usually would prescribe for morning sickness, benza-something, had been removed from the market because of possible side effects; i.e., birth defects. He then explained that the medicine was basically the same ingredients found in Unisom, the sleep aid, and vitamin B12. So he told me to start taking the combination of those two drugs."

"And did it help?"

"It allowed me to get through the day without dry heaves, but it did not relieve my nausea nor my feeling of being hung over. But at least I didn't wake up every fucking morning throwing my guts up."

"This is making you very angry, isn't it?" she asked.

"It's just a very painful memory—the sickness, the pregnancy, the guilt I have about Caroline's birth defect."

"Yes, let's get back to that. Why do you think you had a part in that? Seems to me she had a birth defect, which is why you were sick your entire pregnancy."

"Was it that, or was it from the meds? I will never know. All I know is that when I went back in for my seven-month check-up, the doctor was mortified that I was still taking the Unisom. He told me to get off of it. So I did. Or at least I tried."

"Tried? How so?" She seemed puzzled.

"I foolishly believed the package when it said 'not habit-forming.' I had never taken drugs of any sort, unless Midol counted, so I had no idea that you can't quit 'cold turkey' after being on something for six months. I experienced firsthand what an addict goes through from withdrawal."

I quit taking the sleeping aid that night and had all the withdrawal symptoms: the shivers, the sweats, the shakiness, nausea. It was one of the worst experiences I have ever encountered. I had to go back on Unisom and cut the pills in sections and wean myself off them that way."

"That was wise."

"Walk a mile in my shoes, is all I have to say to anyone who criticizes something they have no firsthand knowledge about." I shivered at the memory.

"What happened afterward?"

"You know, I merely survived. I was miserable and sick and had to take care of a 2-year-old. All I know is that the morning after Caroline was born, it was the first day in nine months I didn't wake up nauseated. It was a blessing. I finally felt relief and then boom—four months later—I found out about her birth defect."

"Why did it take so long to diagnose? And what kind of birth defect did she have?"

"Funny, but it took me almost ten years to call it a birth defect; I guess I was in denial. She had a condition called craniosynostosis. It's where the sutures of the skull are fused together at different points, not allowing the natural growth of the brain; thereby, the skull is misshapen and deformed."

It's like a catch-22. At any rate, my pediatrician discovered it and sent us to Scottish Rite for a CAT scan, and sure enough, she was right. Carrie had the deformity.

"I'll never forget that 'well' visit. It was for her three-month shots, but for some reason, we didn't get in until her fourth month. Anyway, my parents were out of the country, otherwise my mother would have been there with me. Lydia was in Montessori school, and I took Caroline by myself. I was sitting in the room when the nurse measured her head, then she looked at me and left abruptly. She came back in with Dr. G, our pediatrician, who then measured the head.

"They both left the room together, which I thought was very odd. Then they came back into the examination room and explained their concern. I don't remember much else, except the nurse saying: 'It may not seem comforting now, but if your child has to have a birth defect, this is the one you want.' I was dumbfounded. I remember leaving the office, calling Mike, and then heading to my parents' house. Even though they were gone, I didn't want to go home. I cried, called one of my sorority sisters—Nancy, I think— and then called the pediatric neurosurgeon suggested by my pediatrician. The next thing I know, we are making plans for Carrie to have a part of her skull removed. She turned 5 months old in the hospital."

"That must have been horrific." She looked genuinely sad.

"You have no idea. We called both sets of parents. Mine had to fly back from Venice, or wherever they were. His drove up from Florida . . . and the look on Mike's mother's face when she saw my Caroline. She was such a bitch to me. Did I mention I hated his mother? Anyway, she took one look at Carrie in my arms and then said, 'How could you not look at her and see her head was deformed?' Well, I had been seeing her every day for four months and didn't notice the subtle changes. Maybe, if she had been a good grandparent, she would have visited more often. Sorry, old wounds.

"Anyway, the doctor tells us he must do surgery right away and that it was common practice now to ask people you know to donate blood in case something went wrong in surgery and 'Did we want to ask friends to donate?' Caroline had type O blood, the same as Mike. Lydia and I were type A. But my friends with type O blood and who volunteered to donate were, for some reason, told no. Mike wouldn't let any of them donate. He insisted he was the only one to donate blood for her surgery."

"Is this significant?" she asked, already guessing that it was.

"The morning of the surgery we arrived at the hospital at six a.m. My parents were there, as was my Aunt Gail—she drove in from Athens. The doctor greeted us then started to explain that, for some reason, the blood Mike donated was not usable, and did we want to postpone the surgery? Well, I didn't. We had prepared mentally for this, and I wanted to get it over with.

"Mike went totally silent. I had no idea why. I didn't read anything into the fact that his blood was not usable. I just assumed his blood was contaminated or improperly stored or full of vodka. I didn't know nor care. I just wanted to move ahead with the surgery as scheduled.

"Turns out, Mike did read something into the fact that his blood couldn't be used. He took the news that his blood wasn't a match to Carrie, not that there might have been something wrong with his blood. I found out months later he thought Caroline wasn't his . . . Such an egotistical, maniacal man!

God, this makes me hate him all over again! Actually, it's not hate anymore. What is the opposite of love? Indifference? That's what I feel toward him now. But back then, I truly hated him."

"I am beginning to see why," she said.

"Here, our 4-month-old daughter is about to undergo brain surgery, and all he could think of was that the child wasn't his. Men are so fucking selfish. He was an idiot. He ruined everything with his jealousy. I was prepared to stay in the marriage for the sake of the kids, hoping things would get better. You don't know how many people asked me why, if he treated me the way I said, did I have another child with him. And the answer was because I was in it for the long haul. But his insane jealousy was the real reason for the split. Anyway, after Carrie's surgery, we came home and tried to keep up appearances."

"How did the surgery go?"

"It was successful, but I was not prepared for the aftermath. When they unwrapped and removed the bandages from around her head in the hospital, I thought I would faint. She had forty-four staples in her beautiful small head. It looked exactly like the stitching on a softball. I was afraid to touch her, to hold her. I collapsed. I will never forgive myself for my reaction. But I didn't want to hurt her. Gently, we placed her in the car seat and drove her home. The doctors and nurses failed to prepare me for what to expect after her bandages were removed. I cradled her in my arms and rocked her before I put her in her crib. The hospital only sent us home with Tylenol, so I followed the instructions and gave her the medicine. I tried to get some sleep, but she moaned the whole night. Not a loud cry of a 5-month-old baby, but the low, slow moan of someone in true pain.

"They had her on morphine in the hospital and then sent us home with Tylenol. I was dumbfounded, so I called my cousin's husband, Barry, who is a doctor, and he said to ask her doctor for Lortab. So I did. It helped. But the next day, her head was so swollen that her eyes were swollen shut. She looked like a monster." I gasped involuntarily; I couldn't help it. I couldn't help her.

"I had one dear friend who came to see us after we came home from the hospital. She walked into the house, took one look at the baby in my arms, then said, 'I'm sorry. I can't stay.' She literally turned around and ran out of the house."

"My goodness, *that* was a strong reaction." Dr. H was genuinely surprised.

"It was painful to see the reaction from people, but not as painful as it was for Caroline. She was a sweet, innocent infant one day, and a swollen, stapled monster the next. She didn't sleep much after that. She was an active child who never took a nap. She was always into everything. I couldn't keep her mind occupied. I even wrote a couple children's poems about her antics. I will bring them in and let you read them." I laughed out loud when I thought about "the big salad" incident. I would have to share that story with her.

"She was an interesting child: smart, fun, always happy to help. She is more like me than Lydia. Yet, they both remind me of myself in some ways. I love my girls so very much. It's the reason I do not regret marrying Mike. They are smart, fun, and beautiful and the reason I left those bad marriages."

"You mean the reason you left their dad?"

"And Bill, but I don't want to talk about him now."

"And the reason being?"

"He was jealous of Caroline . . . and she almost died. I once again stayed too long with an abusive man, and she paid the price by almost losing her life."

I closed my eyes and thought of the song I used to sing to the girls at bedtime to comfort them and let it comfort me now.

Chapter 18

I Quit You Instead

It was colder than normal, at least for the South. Christmas was around the corner, but the gray of January seemed to have already set in. When it comes to my moods, I am a reflection of the weather. I am a native Southerner who was brought up to bask in the sun before we realized what SPF meant or the damage that can be done by absorbing too much natural vitamin D. I don't mind the rain, as long as I don't have to be out in it. In fact, I love the sound the rain makes when it falls against the window. I don't mind the cold, as long as it is accompanied by the sun. It's these gray days that get me down. What was it Holly Golightly called it? "The mean reds"? Maybe that's why I wore red that day? Black leather pants and a red cashmere turtleneck sweater from Neiman Marcus's signature collection. It's as old as the story I am about to tell.

"Lunch should be allowed," I started as soon as she sat down across from me.

"In what context are you speaking?" She asked, curious as to the start of our conversation.

"In the context that it was because of the fact I had a 'working lunch' with a male colleague that I finally ended my marriage to Mike." I used my fingers to emphasize the quote marks.

"Go on," she said simply.

"It was in August, toward the end of summer."

"What year are you referring to?" Dr. H asked for clarification.

"This was 1997," I answered. "The girls were out of school, so I was home with them that morning. I had gone to work for the City of Fayetteville, which is about twenty miles south of Atlanta, and where I began my life with Mike. It was only part time, directing their Main Street program, which was a national program launched by the National Trust for Historic Preservation. I had been asked by a girlfriend of mine, who was married to one of the councilmen, to help the city by writing the application that would be submitted to the state to get Main Street status. So I took the project on, and when they were awarded the honor of being a Main Street city, the mayor and council asked me if I would take the position and head the department.

"Of course—and the city didn't know this—I was not 'allowed' to work, but for some reason Mike couldn't come up with a valid argument for me not to take the position I was offered. I told the city I would take the job, but that it couldn't interfere with my family; meaning I could work part-time when the girls were in school. I had to continue being both of their room mothers; had to be home when they were home. I truly believe Mike put so many "restrictions" on my acceptance because he didn't think the city would go for it. But they did, so I did. It was a much-needed escape. I needed something for myself—some validation that I could still contribute to society as well as the security of funds for myself. It wasn't much money, but it was mine. All mine.

"Anyway, it was summer, and the girls and I were home. Part of my job description was to assist with economic development, which included saving and restoring the historic homes and buildings in the city. I was working with our local The Home Depot, who generously agreed to renovate our old train depot. They provided all the paint and carpet and the labor. The city got a renovated depot for free. I was in charge of the project.

"The manager of The Home Depot, I think his name was Phillip, called me at home on this particular day. He had just received the plans for the renovation and wanted to take me to lunch to go over them. Well, I didn't see anything wrong with this. It was my job, and it was a generous offer from one of the city's leading businesses, so I told him I would meet him. I called my go-to babysitter and had her come down to watch the girls, and I left for my lunch meeting.

"When I arrived home about an hour and a half later, Mike's car was in the driveway. It seems he called the house, and when the babysitter answered, he was furious that I was at lunch and not home. So he came home from his office, sent the babysitter away, and he waited for me.

"I was nervous when I pulled onto the street and saw his car in the driveway, but this time I did not panic. I opened the door, walked into the kitchen, and waited for his tirade."

"And was it as bad as you expected?" she asked.

"It was worse. He was literally bug-eyed with jealousy. He was standing in the kitchen when I walked in, and his first words were: 'You are not allowed to get a babysitter and go to lunch. In fact, you have to quit that job.'

"I didn't cry, or panic, or raise my voice. I simply answered him: 'I quit you instead.'"

"And what was his response?"

"I really don't remember. I only know that, at that moment, I was finally done. I was through with being bullied, manipulated, emotionally blackmailed, and mentally abused. The marriage was over a long time ago, but I'd reached the point where I had no feelings, only numbness. So I went to the bedroom, changed out of my work suit, and went back into the family room where I gathered the girls and took them outside to play."

"He had never seen me so calm and unafraid. Honestly, looking back, I cannot remember how it all unfolded. It ended for me that day, at that moment. He, of course, tried to talk and say I didn't have to quit my job, but it didn't matter. I told him I was not quitting my job, that I was quitting him. I wanted a divorce, and I was not going to live in a cage anymore.

"I thought back over all the times he manipulated me. Just that July I had produced an important concert for the city with a Garth Brooks impersonator. It was the July Jam, and I had to be at the city square to set up the event at eight a.m. By the time the concert started at eight p.m., Mike was ready to go, and he told me I had to come with him. When I told him I couldn't leave until the stage was removed, he embarrassed me in front of all the people I worked with, shouting that I was his wife and if he told me to come home, then that's what I was to do. Some of the guys that I worked with stepped in and told me to go with him. But I defied him, and I paid for it dearly. But I was willing to pay the price for his injustices toward me. That was the difference in me.

"I was through with being a trophy wife by the end of the summer. And from the moment he told me I had to quit my job, I didn't care what he did, or said, or yelled, or cried. I went on about my business, ignoring him and not giving him the time of day. I treated him with the same indifference he had treated me for ten years. And he couldn't stand it.

"He moved out. It was the Monday after Princess Diana died. I remember because I stayed in bed that entire weekend when she passed. I don't know if I was mourning her or my marriage; it didn't matter. It was over, and he moved out. I carried on as best I could."

"How did the girls take it?" she inquired.

"They were only 5 and 8; Mike really didn't do much with them, so it was not very different. I don't know where he went that day when he finally left. I do know that he was the one who said: 'If you really want this divorce, then let's tell the girls.' When I said, 'OK,' he was shocked. He called them down from their playroom, and we all sat at the kitchen table.

"We had agreed that we were only going to tell them that we decided Daddy should live in another house. But when the girls came down, and I told them he was going to be living on his own, Mike blurted out, 'Mommy doesn't love me anymore and is making me leave.'"

"How did they respond to that?" she asked.

"They both looked at me with questions in their eyes; I was furious. I don't know what I said, but I knew what I was going to be up against. Caroline said, 'OK. Bye, Daddy' and went back upstairs to play. Lydia cried a little and stayed by my side. Then she went out on the front steps to watch him drive away. I was in the kitchen when she came in and got me and said, 'Mommy, he's not leaving.'

"I went outside on the front porch area with her and sure enough, he had parked his car in the guest parking space in the front of the house. Then he gets out of the car and about halfway up the walk, gets down on his knees and crawls to me, begging me to take him back.

"I was dumbfounded and numb and furious that he did that in front of Lydia. I looked at him and said, 'No.' I walked back inside, closed the door, and left him out in front of the house on his knees.

"I don't know what happened next or how long he stayed out there, but a couple of minutes went by, and Lydia came inside and announced he was gone and then went upstairs to play with Caroline.

"I took them out to dinner at their favorite wing restaurant in the city and read to them before I tucked them into bed. I slept well that night and all the nights after. I never looked back. No matter how many people told me to go back or to let him come home—I stood my ground."

"You were stronger than you thought," she suggested.

"No. It took all of my strength and courage to stand up to him. He was a bully and an abuser, and I didn't want my girls to grow up with that image of their mother. And I was a good mother."

"And how is your relationship with the girls today?" she asked.

"That's an entirely different chapter of my life; two more, to be exact."

I left Dr. H's office knowing my journey with her was only half over. I had dug up so many things buried deep in the past, things I never thought I would have to revisit. But I did and with that, I felt a sense of relief. Of letting go. There was still Bill and New York and the end of another marriage to remember. I needed time to decide if I could go down that path with her—the hurt was closer to the surface with these than the other memories. They were perhaps still too fresh, like a wound that had just begun to scab over. I didn't know if I wanted it to heal up completely or if I was ready to scratch it off and watch it bleed again.

Chapter 19
Dinner is Best Served Cold

I was wearing a red cashmere sweater dress with thigh-high black boots. I needed this session for a multitude of reasons. Talking about the girls' dad, bringing up all the old wounds, emotions, and trauma was probably not a good idea this time of year.

It was early winter, and I understood why it is the season most people take their own lives. It was cold and gray, depressing and unkind. It's supposed to be "the most wonderful time of the year," and it is for those who are happy. But for those of us who are holding on by a cashmere thread, struggling to get out of our Horchow bed, it can be an endless trigger.

I will admit that I did love Christmas, even when I was struggling to pay my bills and buy my gifts. I loved to give; it makes me truly happy. It's true, it is better to give than to receive. So when I couldn't afford to give gifts at Christmas, it was yet another reason for me to feel depressed. I scheduled this appointment with Dr. H before she left for the holidays and after one of the most bizarre nights of my life, which is saying a lot.

"I'm glad we could work you in," she began. "Is everything all right or are you just anxious about the upcoming holiday?"

"A little bit of both, I guess." I lied.

She no longer required a letter or quote or poem from me, and I hadn't prepared anything. So I started to tell her about the party I had attended the Saturday night before.

"I went to a dinner party this past weekend," I began, "and I am still trying to process the events that unfolded."

"Sounds interesting." She was all ears.

"I run in a certain circle, as they say, that is quite high-brow in *The New Yorker* cartoon sort of way," I said by way of explanation. "In fact, I have many circles in which I travel, but this one is by far the most entertaining with the most interesting characters.

"First, there is Anne Brooks, or AB as her closest friends refer to her. She is from a very wealthy family, in the vein of F. Scott Fitzgerald's definition. She was the hostess for the dinner party that was to be a sort of 'Welcome to Atlanta' for D, the lead singer from a well-known group formed in the late seventies," I paused, "who happens to be gay." He was a dear old friend of one of the other guests, Berkeley, who is, shall we say, an enigma in every sense of the word.

"Berkeley collects many things: knick-knacks and oddities of all kinds, including men. Gay, straight, bi—but always rich and famous. She was a model and a muse to musicians, moguls, and movie stars. She was photographed by Helmut Newton in the seventies, his black and white photographs of her, in various degrees of nudity, hang on her bedroom walls in her house on Habersham. Of course, this being the South, she puts small yellow sticky notes on the areas of questionable taste. She is the ultimate trophy wife and is married to Gus, whose jealously rears its head whenever he feels threatened by her outside world. She calls him "Gaslight Gus," for he will do anything to embarrass her so no one will have anything to do with her—all the while making her think she is the one at fault. She is the epitome of a trophy, and he is the epitome of a narcissist.

"Meanwhile, back at the party," Dr. H made a joke.

"Yes, back to the party guest list. There's me, of course, and AB, the hostess, her next-door neighbors, Rob and CJ. Then there was Berkeley and her famous friend D along with two other fabulous gentlemen from Atlanta, Don Purcel and Thom Baker, and I kid you not, a former circus performer whose last name was Tangle. To answer the most-asked question, he was a sword swallower. Oh, and my dear friend Ellen, the statuesque redhead who was the youngest one at the dinner, with the exception of Mr. Tangle, who at 24 was the youngest in age but under no circumstances the most naïve.

"Since I knew the guest list, I felt comfortable in my selection of wardrobe for the evening, which was a short, tight black knit skirt and a camel V-neck knit top that came just far enough down in the front and far enough down in the back to show off my curves. Oh, and since all the men at the dinner were gay, with the exception of dear old Rob, I didn't bother to wear a bra."

"This is important, because. . . ?" She let the last word linger.

"It's important because I felt free to be me and not wear anything under my clothes. But it turned out to be a dangerous decision. For, you see, what no one expected or predicted was that Berkeley's husband, Gus, who *never* goes out of his house, came to the dinner, uninvited, with Berkeley."

"I am assuming that this changed the entire dynamic of the dinner party?"

"You have no idea," I said as I recrossed my legs. "Berkeley came in with Gus, apologizing, saying that he simply insisted on coming. Because he wasn't expected, Berkeley brought in two bags of Chick-fil-A, which she said was to be his dinner. AB, being the consummate host that she was, asked her house manager to set another place at the table. She then turned to Gus and welcomed him to her home.

"At which point, Gus, who was in Vietnam and has the Purple Heart car tag to prove it, told her he brought her a little hostess gift."

"Which was?" Dr. H asked.

"A gun," I answered.

"A gun?"

"Yes, a real, live gun. And a box of ammunition."

"I don't know what to say."

"Neither did any of us, except AB, who simply said, 'Why thank you, Gus. I appreciate you thinking of me.'"

"What was everyone else's response?"

"We just all stood in the kitchen and watched as the event unfolded in disbelief," I told her. "It was very early in the evening. Little did I know that as the evening wore on, things were going to get 'curiouser and curiouser'. . .

"AB had asked me to take on the responsibility of accepting people's coats as they came in and to put them in the library, so after the 'gun as a hostess gift' incident, I was happy to have an excuse to leave the cocktail reception as often as I could.

"D's friend, Mr. Tangle, arrived, and I took his coat from him and walked from the kitchen area, through the family room, into the entry hall, and up the few stairs that led to the library just before you went into the master wing."

"Sounds like a very nice house," she mused.

"Like Fitzgerald said, 'The rich are different from you and me.' Anyway, I placed the coat on the dark leather sofa and turned to walk out of the library when I was met by Gus, my oldest and dearest friend's husband, on the landing. He was just standing there, waiting for me. It still gives me the shivers, even now, when I picture how he was just standing there, in wait.

"I said something like, 'Are you looking for the powder room?' and he just stared at me. Remember, I was wearing a low-cut, thin sweater with no bra or nipple covers, and it was a cold night. I was thinking that there would be no straight men attending the dinner.

"Gus just grins at me then makes me a proposition. He says he will give me a thousand dollars if he can, and I quote, 'see your tits.' I was totally caught off guard and just stood there. He starts to put his hand in his pocket for his wallet, when he realizes he did not bring it with him. He then asks me to wait on the landing and promises he will be right back.

"From my angle on the landing, I can see into the family room and into the kitchen, where he goes and asks his wife, Berkeley, something. She goes to her purse, pulls out her wallet, and hands him some cash. He comes back to me on the landing and says, 'I only have $300 tonight, but if you come by my house tomorrow, I can give you the rest of the money and you can show them to me then.'"

"You really can't make this up, can you?" Dr. H asked, her head shaking.

"Um, no."

"What did you do?" she asked.

"Well, first you have to understand that Gus is a very peculiar man, and I have heard similar stories about his behavior and his obsession with women. Plus, he had just brought a gun to a dinner party and offered it to the host as a gift, so I was not about to do anything to upset him. I took the $300, then waited for him to join the party. I walked to the hallway nearest the kitchen and motioned for Berkeley. When she met me in the entry hall, I told her exactly what had just transpired. I gave her the money back and told her, emphatically, that I would not be coming to the house tomorrow to collect the other money, nor would I be showing him my breasts."

"And her response?"

"She simply shook her head, said something about wondering why he had asked her for money, and then thanked me for letting her know and for giving her back the money. Then she told me what a good friend I was to her and ended our conversation by saying she wondered how many other friends of hers he had made the same offer to and they didn't tell her.

"We both agreed that I would sit on one side of Gus and she on the other during dinner so he could not make a play at young, beautiful, naïve Ellen."

"That's quite a story," she stated.

"Oh, it doesn't end there," I laughed a sly little laugh. "I hear a piano play-ing coming from the other side of the entry from the music room. I decide to follow it instead of going back into the kitchen to face Gus and the other guests.

"Turns out it's Mr. Tangle, playing beautifully as Ellen sits listening. I apologize for my intrusion, and then Ellen, wide-eyed, says, oh no, you must come sit with me and let Reese tell his story.

"Seems Mr. Tangle is from a family of gypsies who were all in the circus. They had an act, somewhere in the Midwest I think, and he was one of sev-eral brothers who became adept at sword swallowing, thanks to his uncles who would force them to perform fellatio on them when they were young. He also was adept at twisting his body into different positions, which is how he found himself invited to the dinner party after D discovered him as he performed at one of the local gay clubs. Oh, and he also swallowed fire."

"Oh my," was all she replied.

"Oh my, indeed. It was around nine p.m. before we were led into the din-ing room and found our seats at the table. I, as instructed, took the seat next to Gus's left, as Berkeley took the one to his right. I knew which seat was Gus's since it was the only plate with Chick-fil-A sandwiches and waffle fries piled on the Limoges porcelain.

"With Ellen seated on my left, in between Mr. Tangle and me and out of arm's reach of Gus, we eat our salads, drink our wine, and try to make polite conversation, as you do. I can't really remember how the topic came up, but we started talking about favorite movies and why we chose them. Someone mentioned *The Big Lebowski*, I think it was Rob. And Gus, who had not really done or said anything at dinner, except try to feel me up under the table and stare at Ellen while Berkeley tried to control the situation, decided to tell a story. And oh, what a story it was.

"Seems he had a dominatrix-slash-mistress in New York City who he insisted was the model for the character played by Julianne Moore in *The Big*

Lebowski. He then proceeds, during the main dinner course, to tell how she would tie him up in her loft and swing from the ceiling as she assaulted him with a rubber dildo. He went into such graphic detail that we all just sat in shock after he was finished.

"Then, Mr. Tangle leans into Ellen and me and asks, 'Should I tell him my sword swallowing story?' At which point she and I say in unison, an emphatic *no*."

"What happened after that?" the doctor asked.

"I am really not quite sure; I think AB said something like, 'Well that was quite the story,' then she changed the subject. We had our dessert and coffee, and then Don and Thom walked me to the door and I left."

"I have no words," she said as she shook her head.

"I found out later that the insanity continued after my departure until Gus literally fell out of the house onto the driveway and landed in the bushes before getting in his Mercedes and heading home, his job of completely taking over the dinner party complete.

"I guess the rich are different, but then again, who's to say what's normal? Maybe it's the rich who are normal and the rest of us are just trying to play along in a world that has no tolerance for the weak."

I pondered my last statement, proud of the fact that I was able to break my pattern of passiveness and stand up for myself. But was it because of my loyalty to a friend, or was I starting to recognize my worth as a person and not as an object? I grabbed my leopard print coat, put it on over my red cashmere dress, and made my way out into the shortest cold day of the season.

Chapter 20
Curiouser and Curiouser

It was a Wednesday, and I almost canceled on Dr. H. I had been trying to write something about Bill, but the words were not flowing like usual. For inspiration, I went to my complete works of Shakespeare, the small faded blue books that my mother gave me as a gift for my birthday many years ago, but I found none. People who truly know me know that books are my favorite gift to give and to receive—especially books of poetry. My cousin Terry gave me leather-bound books by famous poets as a Christmas gift one year. I received several volumes and placed them proudly in the Montrose house family room on the library shelves that flanked the fireplace. I would take a volume down and read from the pages, at first finding my favorite familiar poems, like "Ode on a Grecian Urn" by John Keats. I can still recite the last line in my mind: "Beauty is truth, truth beauty, that is all Ye know on earth, and all ye need to know."

I wanted to bring in a poem that might explain my time with Bill, but I couldn't find the right one, and I had not been able to summon the right words to write my own.

"And who are we talking about today?" she asked.

Strange. I am distracted by her outfit today. She was in a navy blue pantsuit with white cotton blouse, the kind of outfit you buy from Belk's when you have a parent-teacher conference and you want to be taken seriously.

"They say that people come into your life for a reason, a season, or a life-time," I began. "And I almost canceled . . . "

"Why?" she asked.

"Because I was planning on talking about Bill."

"Finally," she said.

"Why do you say that?" I was confused. *How does she know my storyline with Bill?* And then I remembered. *Oh, yes, the* AJC *newspaper article from last year—the one that chronicled his rise and fall in Atlanta.* I sometimes forget that I was married to a quasi-celebrity.

"He was the love of my life, or so I thought. All the others before him and after could never compare to the love we shared. He loved me for me and didn't want to change me. He embraced my sense of style, loved my sense of humor, and told me every day how much he loved me.

"He was a 'man about town' in New York, had his own entertainment show on CNN, went to all the movie premieres and after-parties, the Oscars— you name it. He was a very eligible bachelor in the best city in the world, and he fell in love with *me*."

"From what I see, there is a lot to love about you."

This invoked a semi-smile, but I ignored the comment. "I was a single mother of two daughters with a monster of an ex-husband who tormented me. Bill came into my life at the right time. He stood up to Mike when I couldn't. He was a great stepfather and a wonderful husband, lover, and friend. And then . . . he wasn't."

"What happened?"

"Life happened," I responded. "He was alive and well and living in New York, and then he retired from CNN and from himself. But it was my decision to move back to Atlanta, and that's when he stopped living. I took him out of his element."

"According to the newspaper article, he became an alcoholic and basically lost everything. Including you," she said.

Aha. She knew more about me and about Bill than she let on.

"It wasn't an overnight thing. It was more like a gradual descent into madness. And it was very painful to witness. Once again, I stayed too long. That's my real problem. That damned eternal optimist in me refuses to let go or give up or accept defeat. I hang on until there is nothing left but memories and milestones."

"That sounds like a fairy tale," she smiled.

"More like a country song," I responded, and then I started to tell her all about Bill.

"Bill really brought out my sexuality. I was always a 'sexual' person, and I know what you're going to say. Yes, probably because I was molested, but I also think it is who I am naturally. He was a very handsome man. Tall, lean, with a wicked sense of humor. I remember watching him on Ted Turner's Channel 17 when I was growing up in Atlanta. I had the biggest crush on him. All my friends did at the time. He was the biggest celebrity in Atlanta. And then he moved away, and I lost track . . . until he came back into my life.

"I had literally signed my divorce papers from the girls' dad and swore I would never get married again. It was a Friday in January 1998. I was still the Main Street program director and PR person for the City of Fayetteville, still working part-time so I could be home with the girls. It was a very sad time for me, for I was broken and battered and bruised. My mother was not supportive of my choice to divorce, and therefore I was on my own emotionally. In fact, when I married Bill, she didn't even come to my wedding in Palm Springs. But my sisters, aunt, cousins, and girlfriends were there for me."

"She didn't come to your wedding?" she asked.

"No, and it still hurts me to this day." I remembered just how hurt I was, how betrayed I felt by my own mother. "She didn't approve of me divorcing the father of my children. And she was not impressed that I had met a celebrity. In fact, when I told her I had met Bill Tush, her response was, 'Isn't he married to Connie Sellecca?'" I laughed, realizing that my mother thought I was referring to John Tesh.

"How did you meet him?"

"I was going to the Fayette County Chamber of Commerce banquet—the Saturday after I signed my divorce papers—with my girlfriend Tami and her husband. The guy they were trying to set me up with got stuck in a snowstorm out west in some Harley Davidson town, so I was going solo. Bill was the guest speaker, and I hadn't thought of him in twenty years. I didn't know it at the time, but he had picked me out of the crowd when I entered the room. He was sitting at the bar observing all the people, he told me later. He said he immediately saw me and was attracted to me—to my legs, to be exact. But he figured this was Atlanta and everyone down here was married.

"After Bill's speech, I made my way through the crowd to tell him how much I enjoyed his talk, and I did. He was just as funny and entertaining as I had remembered. He asked me to join him for a drink, and I did. Everyone kept coming up to speak to him, but he kept touching my hand as if to say I was the only one in the room."

"Sounds like he was smitten." Dr. H broke her silence.

"I think we both were," I responded. "Anyway, the couple I came with were leaving, and Bill asked me if I could stay. What I thought was a one-night stand turned into a twelve-year marriage. I thought I could have my fling with my girlhood crush who would then go back to New York, and I would go on with my boring life in little Fayetteville, Georgia."

"But it didn't turn out that way?" she asked, knowing the answer.

"No. He told me I was everything he had ever wanted in a woman. Cliche, I know. But we had instant chemistry. Tami called me the next morning to pick me up from his hotel. Bill asked if I could take him to the airport. I remember getting into her car early that Sunday morning in my cocktail dress and trench coat from the night before, and she was playing Frank Sinatra's 'Strangers in the Night.' Funny, it became our song. Anyway, I go home, take a quick shower, and return to pick him up and drive him to the airport. He gets my number and kisses me goodbye. I drive to church, pick up the girls from my sister Jennifer, and then go by KFC for takeout. The girls are eating, and I am resting, since I didn't get much sleep the night before. The phone rings, and it's Bill calling from the airplane on those phones they used to have in the seats. Remember this is 1998."

"Were you surprised you heard from him?" she asked.

"Yes, especially so early and from the plane. I guess I assumed I would never hear from him again. Turns out, he couldn't stop thinking about me. He flew me up to New York the following weekend, and nine months later we were married."

"I'm guessing the nine months in between were magical?" she responded, and I think, *Is she as caught up in my fairytale as the rest of Atlanta was?*

"You have no idea." I stopped to think about whether I was going to tell her about those months. *Will she believe it?* My own version of *Fifty Shades of Grey*. I still have moments of doubt, and I sometimes find myself reliving those experiences when I am all alone at night in my king-size bed and can't seem to fall asleep. I replay them over and over in my mind, even though it takes me to a time I felt out of control, like Alice passing through the looking glass, falling down the rabbit's hole, into the well filled with cupboards and bookshelves, into the unknown.

Chapter 21
Sweet Emotion

Some stories are easier to tell, like childhood recollections of family milestones permanently embedded in our collective memories thanks to faded photographs and Polaroids placed in well-worn albums. They roll off your tongue as easily as *y'all* or *fixin' to* or *bless her heart* does in the deep South.

And then there is this one.

It began so innocently yet ends up *so* not. It is the story of lust and longing and what I thought to be love in a sort of *Basic Instinct* sense. Turns out, it was love, but it took me on a strange path to find it.

I handed Dr. H my handwritten note, then spoke the words out loud. They were two quotes from Lewis Carroll's *Alice's Adventures in Wonderland*:

> Either the well was very deep, or she fell very slowly, for she had plenty of time as she went down to look about her, and to wonder what was going to happen next.

> It's no use going back to yesterday, because I was a different person then.

She nodded her head as if to say she remembered the quotes well, then I began our session.

"It had been three months of Bill flying me up to New York every other weekend before I discovered what the city was all about." I was remembering the first time I realized how different a world could be from the reserved one I knew in small-town Fayetteville, Georgia.

"What happened that opened your eyes?" she asked.

"Elissa happened." I stated matter-of-factly.

"Elissa being?"

"Elissa was a 22-year-old Hawaiian Tropic model who, in true narcissist style, took Bill up on his offer to stay at his NYC penthouse whenever she was in the city. Bill had been a judge in the Miss Hawaiian Tropic contest for several years, being a friend of the owner of the company. He would fly to Hawaii for a week, stay in an oceanfront resort, and render his decision—of the one hundred or so contestants, only four finalists are selected to go to Vegas for the final competition.

"Being a Miss Hawaiian Tropic judge had a lot of advantages. Especially if you were an eligible bachelor who happened to have a TV show covering the entertainment world for a major cable network. Needless to say, membership into that exclusive club had many, many privileges.

"For most of the one hundred girls from all over the U.S. who had probably won their coveted role in Miss Hawaiian Tropic as a bikini-clad contestant in a dive bar called 'Wagon Wheels' or 'Flipflops,' the chance to go to Hawaii to compete in a bathing suit for a week was very tempting. These girls ranged in age from 18 to 30, were nipped, tucked, bleached, and for the most part, stunning. Some were short, some were tall, but they all had incredible bodies. All tanned. All these girls knew the power of the P, and if they didn't know how to use it before the Miss Hawaiian Tropic model competition, they certainly *left* there knowing."

I paused when I noticed she was scribbling as fast as she could and allowed her time to catch up on documenting all the decadent details of my story. I wondered to myself if there really are complete guarantees of confidentiality, knowing that I have been privy to private conversations between professionals. I was reminded, again, of the words of Benjamin Franklin who said, "Three may keep a secret, if two of them are dead."

"The judges were a mix of celebrities, semi-famous people, and sponsors. Bill fell into the semi-famous category. But when you put the judge badge on, it leveled the playing field. And play they did.

"Well-known football heroes with wives and kids back home would awkwardly slip away the morning after the final competition, so they wouldn't have to say goodbye to the model they had played with the entire week. One football legend, who later would be arrested and tried for the murder of his wife, became incensed and threw a fit when only three of the four models he wanted to go back to his room would participate. Notoriously sleazy predators were also known to judge for many years before winding up behind bars or in a bar throwing around their badges and taking no prisoners.

"It was quite the scene, and I had the honor of being a judge myself later in our marriage. It was during this time I realized these were the kind of girls who go after—and get—what they want, using all the resources God gave them. They were smart, sly, and cunning, and winners at all costs."

And I was a naive thirty-something mother of two when I was introduced into this world, I think to myself.

"And Elissa?" She prompted me to continue on my original train of thought.

"Elissa ended up being the catalyst in our relationship, the Miss Hawaiian Tropic model contestant who found herself living in Bill's spare bedroom in the NYC penthouse during most of our courtship."

"And you didn't have a problem with this arrangement?"

"I was taken aback at first. But then you have to understand that I, in all honesty, am not a jealous person. I may not like something, but very rarely do I get jealous. If someone I am dating wants to go out with someone else, then I have no problem with that . . . just know I will do the same.

"Elissa was different. She was young and opportunistic; she was a statuesque brunette with dark eyes, very exotic. She was from the Midwest, but not like anything I'd ever seen produced from that region. Bill and I used to have a running joke: Whenever we were at an airport we would play the game 'lesbian or Midwesterner?' Elissa would not have fallen into either category. I think her mother was Spanish and her father Swedish from Michigan, so she was quite the mix. She was arrogant and fun, and it made for quite the combination."

"So you were just beginning to date this man, who happened to be on TV and had a Hawaiian Tropic model living in his apartment, and you had no problem with this arrangement?" Dr. H seemed perplexed.

"I know it sounds strange, but I really had no right to say anything about the arrangement. As it turned out, Bill, who was turning 50, was pretty boring when it came to nightlife. He would go to his movie premieres and events and do his show live-to-tape from all over the city, then he would head home and watch TV and go to bed by ten p.m. When I would visit, we would end up making dinner and sitting on his love seat watching old movies before going to bed. So when Elissa got there, she was the one with all the hook-ups for underground parties. Bill never was interested in that, I think because he had already been there and done that when he lived in Los Angeles. He had outgrown that scene.

"I, on the other hand, was fascinated by the underground clubs and events that went on after midnight. The ones you had to 'know' about and present a secret phrase just to be allowed in."

"You attended those without him?" She was curious. "How did that go over?"

"It was no problem. I mean, how can you get upset at your girlfriend, who doesn't mind that you have a 22-year-old Hawaiian Tropic model living with you? Not to mention the fact that when I would be in his apartment on a Friday waiting for him to come home from work, I would take messages all day from different girls he had met at different events. He would come home, and I'd hand him a sheet of paper with names and numbers and messages that said: 'I'm in town this weekend and would love to get together if you have the time.' It got to be pretty funny. I didn't mind. I was seeing other guys back home."

"So you were both seeing other people?"

"We were, but we were only sleeping with each other. That was something we both were adamant about."

"You trusted him with that?"

"People always got the wrong impression about Bill. He was actually an old soul who preferred black and white movies or Andy Griffith reruns in the privacy of his apartment to the new blockbuster films and premiere parties he was invited to."

"So he was not the image he portrayed?"

"Yes and no," I answered. "He wasn't the 'man about town' he fashioned himself after. But when it came to sex, he was into a lot of things I had only read about in books."

"So he played to your wild side?"

"Yes, he unleashed it. Or rather, Elissa did."

"As much as I hate to stop here, I have to," she said. "I am interested in learning how you came to realize this other side to your sexuality. But we will have to save that for our next session."

The taboos of my childhood Baptist upbringing, sins such as drinking, dancing, and fornication, were falling into place all around me as I fell down the well of Wonderland. I don't know if I was really ready for it. I don't believe many people are.

Chapter 22
Mother, May I?

I began a double session of therapy since the last one went further than we expected, and I took a moment to adjust my dress. It was a bit shorter than I remembered it being. I purchased it in New York when I needed a new outfit for every occasion and couldn't be caught dead in the same dress. Funny, but in New York one only wears black, so in reality who would notice? Thank God it was before Facebook took off; you can't get away with second helpings of anything now. Not even basic black.

I pulled the Cynthia Rowley out of storage, had it cleaned, and put it in the back of my closet. For some reason I chose to wear it that day. It is black, which should go without saying, with a mock turtleneck closure surrounded by a fake mink Peter Pan collar. The matching jacket has the same fake fur collar and hides the fact that the cut of the dress exposes my bare shoulders. Did it shrink at the cleaners, or did I really wear my dresses this short, I ask myself? At any rate, it showcases my legs, which are bare all the way to my highest Miu Miu peep-toed suede shoes.

I don't know why my hand went to this outfit and my mind said yes. Comfort I suppose? Maybe I needed to feel like my true self to tell my story?

Whatever the reason, I knew that I needed to continue my story as soon as possible in case I lost the courage to dive below the surface. Hence, the double session. These were the rationales going through my mind as I hand Dr. H. my thought of the day.

"I can't go back to yesterday because I was a different person then."

—Lewis Carroll, *Alice in Wonderland*

She read the note then asked, "Are you in so much pain?"

"Define pain?" I asked.

"I think you know the definition to which I refer."

"I am not in that 'gut-wrenching' pain I felt when I tried to end my life," I answered. "But, yes, I am still in pain. Isn't everyone?"

"No. They aren't." She looked at me and for a moment, I thought she was going to get up out of her chair and come over to the couch where I was sitting.

"I've thought about our last session, and then I went rummaging through some old letters . . . and I found this."

I handed Dr. H the private event invitation from the New York nightclub Mother to one of their infamous Tuesday night Jackie 60 parties.

"What is it?"

"It *was* a nightclub in the meatpacking district of New York back in the day. Surely you've heard about these kinds of clubs? I mean, you did watch *Sex and the City*?" I asked. Then I realized, no, not everyone in Normal, USA, realizes these sorts of clubs exist.

"No," she admitted. "I am afraid I have not. Please enlighten me."

"Mother was a club in lower-midtown Manhattan that opened at midnight and went until morning. The meatpacking district was not the Disneyland that it is today, and these clubs were hidden in the bowels of the buildings where animals were slaughtered up above by day, and people were decadently partying like animals down below at night."

I had read about these S&M clubs in novels and in ever-so-informed *Vanity Fair* articles, but this was the first time I had experienced it myself.

"So, Elissa was invited by this editor of *Paper* magazine to come to the Jackie 60 party on the Tuesday I was arriving to visit Bill. It was spring break, and my girls were with their dad, so I took the week off and went to New York. Elissa had been living in his spare room for a good month, and I'd had the chance to get to know her and she'd had the chance to get to know me. In fact, Elissa and I would end up hanging out and drinking champagne on the terrace when Bill would go to bed early.

"The Jackie 60 party didn't even start until midnight, so I knew he wasn't going to go. He didn't mind if I did, and Elissa was happy to have me tag along—especially since this editor was pursuing her . . . and she was pursuing a good time and someone who could provide it. The editor was not too happy about me going; he thought he would have her all to himself. But he warmed up by the time we got to Mother."

I took a sip of my LaCroix, lemon-flavored this time, with no wine additive.

"It was everything I expected and more. We were dropped off in this seedy-looking part of town with butcher shops and cow images on the buildings. It was the meatpacking district, which I found out later would be the location of my favorite NYC restaurant, Pastis. The editor looked at the address—there was no marquee with the word *Mother* on it, but confirmed the building and proceeded down these metal steps until we got to a door. He knocked and this window opened, very *Wizard of Oz*-like, and after the password was confirmed, we were let inside.

"What was the password?" she inquired, rather unexpectedly.

"*Paper cut*, which technically is two words," I told her.

"Anyway, what a shock it was once we were allowed in. All I remember is flocked floral wallpaper, red velvet and male-only waiters dressed like Jackie Kennedy circa 1960, with pastel suits, pillbox hats, and pearl ear-bobs, as my grandmother referred to them. Hence the 'Jackie 60' themed night. I knew I wasn't in Kansas anymore. The bar only served bottled water, which I found out later was because everyone was doing XTC—Ecstasy. Except me, until later that night. We met up with an L.A. fashion designer who was in town, a very large, handsome, built Black man whose name I cannot remember. We all took a hit of XTC, got our water, and jumped on the dance floor.

"I found out later that XTC was supposed to be a 'love' drug. But it did nothing for me. We were all dancing in the main room, when suddenly this circle of Middle Eastern people surrounded me and started dancing. I didn't think anything about it until the L.A. designer literally picked me up and carried me back to our group. He told me to be careful who I dance with, especially that group. I could have been sold . . . or worse!"

She gasped under her breath but didn't say a word. So I continued.

"Just when I thought it couldn't get any stranger, the music stopped, the curtains opened, and everyone's attention was drawn to the performers on stage. There were two men, dressed only in black leather chaps with black leather masks carrying black leather whips."

I noticed that Dr. H's mouth had dropped open; she didn't. So, again, I continued.

"Yes, it was an S&M show . . . but it was when a woman came into the action that I decided the XTC must not be working since I was *way* too sober to watch what was happening right before my eyes. I found Elissa, who was in the unisex bathroom doing who knows what, and I told her I was leaving. She had already ditched the editor, so she went with me.

"It was four a.m., we caught a cab, and we headed back to 34th and 9th Avenue. I came in and went off on Bill for who knows what. Maybe the XTC did have an effect on me, but it was not the desired one. By the way, I have discovered that I get mad on XTC; crazy on absinthe; wild on tequila . . . but then that eventually leads to crazy; and amorous on champagne, which is why I stick to champagne."

"What happened when you came home that leads you to say you went off on Bill?" she asked.

"I just remember coming in at four a.m., waking him up, and giving him a piece of my mind. I don't know why. It is not like me to express my feelings when I am angry. I told you, I was taught to hold in your emotions when you are upset or angry or sad. It's only happy feelings that are allowed to be shown. Those, and love."

"So you think it was this drug that caused you to express your true feelings?"

"It had to be . . . I was always trying to be perfect with him and not show him that anything bothered me. I mean, for Christ's sake, I didn't say a word about the Hawaiian Tropic model living in the spare bedroom. But that's not reality. We had an unpleasant visit. We had only been seeing each other for three months, but I found out later it was Elissa that was bothering me. She was noticing how Bill was starting to really fall for me, and she was afraid that her free place to stay in New York would be short-lived. It's hard to begin a new relationship when you have a five-foot-eleven-inch model sabotaging your every move."

"So was it a calculated move, you and Bill?"

"Not at first. I wasn't really interested in getting married again. But then, in between the times we were together, when I would date other guys, I found myself longing to be with him. That's my problem, I find someone I want to be with, and I want that feeling all the time. So I had to discover what made Bill tick and how to harvest that intel to my advantage."

"You mean to get him to marry you?" She quizzed me now.

"Not necessarily to get him to marry me; I didn't really know what I wanted. I just knew that each time we were together, I fell deeper and deeper in love with him. After he asked me to marry him, he wanted me to come up for two weeks to live with him to see if we could live together. I told him, the question isn't 'Can you live with someone?' The question is 'Can you live without them?' If you can't live without them in your life, then that's the one.

"I had that with my first husband. I married my second husband out of guilt." I paused, waiting for her response. She gave me that "go on" look, and so I did.

"He left his wife and two children for me; I felt obligated. I mean, I think I had feelings for him, but he wasn't the love of my life. And he did give me two very intelligent, beautiful children, but he was so controlling; I should have known better than to believe he would be any different. He showed me his true colors when we were dating. He was holding on so tight. Then he let go and eased up after I fled."

"What do you mean by fled?" she asked.

"He smothered me with flowers, gifts, and trips. He wanted to be with me all the time. At first I thought, *This is great.* Then I felt smothered and started to pull away. I told him I couldn't do this . . . and he listened. He eased up and let me do things with my friends. It wasn't until after the wedding, when I got the *Gone with the Wind* job, that it all fell apart."

"How long was that into your marriage?"

"Exactly one year and two months." I remembered it well. "It was great until it wasn't."

How did I get back on Mike? I asked myself. I prefer to keep my time with him a distant memory.

"Anyway, I don't want to revisit that." I looked at her, and this time she responded.

"You should really be able to talk about that time with Mike here, now, so you can let it go. This is the deep-diving underneath that surface I keep pressing you for."

Chapter 23
V is for Vindication

A narcissist has many weapons at their disposal to use on their victims, the "loves of their lives": exploitation, coercion, mental abuse, lying, cheating, manipulation, projection, deflection, and gaslighting, to name a few. Of these, the mental abuse of manipulation and gaslighting can inflict the most devastating harm and lasting wounds. I often told my mother, after I had left the girls' dad, that I wished he had beaten me—at least she could have seen the bruises, the marks, the indelible damage left on my body. With mental abuse, especially from a narcissist, the damage is hidden deep in the mind and subconscious of its intended victim. But it is there just the same.

I never thought of myself as a victim of mental and emotional abuse until I learned about narcissistic abuse. Then everything fell into place. The love bombing, the gaslighting, the manipulation, the projection of cheating, the devaluation—the only thing Mike failed to do was discard me. At the time, I had no idea there was even such a thing, a "disorder," if you will. But looking back on our relationship, it fits the mold so nicely. His uncontrollable rages, his jealous fits, his silent treatment when I didn't think I had done anything wrong. Couple that with his pathological jealousy, and it was a recipe for disaster. The only question left was whether he realized what he had done. It took some twelve years after I divorced him to find the answer.

"Have I shared with you how I was finally vindicated in regard to my suspicions about the girls' dad and how he treated us?" I asked before Dr. H had the chance to sit down.

"By whom?" She asked.

"By myself," I smiled. "Well, actually, by my daughters. I am proud of the fact that I never said an unkind word about the man who fathered them. I knew it would only make me look bad in their eyes and would make them defensive. So I bit my tongue whenever they would come back from his house repeating the things he would say," I adjusted my long-sleeved floral Moschino dress with the keyhole cutout that skimmed my braless breasts just so, and continued.

"I never wanted to hurt them, so they never heard me say a hateful word about him. After all, he was half of who they were. Nor did I ever try to explain to them the reason I divorced their dad when they were only 5 and 8."

"That's a very positive response to the situation," she told me. "It must have been difficult not to justify yourself when they were asking questions."

"I would never intentionally hurt anyone, especially my girls," I responded. "Besides, how could I explain what a monster their father was to me when I spent the majority of my marriage trying to hide the fact that he was emotionally and mentally abusive?

"I remember after Mike had left our house and moved into an apartment, my mother kept saying to me that if I had a better relationship with the Lord, I could learn to live with him. She was very disappointed in me for not 'learning to live with it' and to stay in my marriage for the sake of the children. After all, 'It's what you do.'

"I was dumbfounded. Turns out he had been calling her, telling her he would do anything to get me back and asking her what he could do. He even called my closest cousin and confidant, Terry. She actually called me trying to talk me into getting back with him.

"I was furious with his campaign to get back into my life. I spent nine years out of our ten-year marriage apologizing to him for whatever it was he perceived I was doing wrong. I never knew what his mood was going to be when he got home. I walked on eggshells in case someone happened to mention to him that they saw me at the grocery store, having lunch, or buying gas, or doing whatever tasks a normal life would require. If he had not known I was going to stop for groceries or lunch or gas, he assumed I was doing something behind his back. It was an impossible situation to live with someone who always assumes the worst.

"So when Mother told me 'perhaps if you had a better relationship with God, you could learn to live with Mike' and keep my family together, I told her ever so bluntly. I said, 'Mother, I do have a great relationship with God. In fact, I pray every night. I say, 'Dear Lord, please let Mike get killed in a car accident on the way home so I won't have to live in this hell.'

"And when he would go pheasant hunting out West or quail hunting down South, I would pray: 'Dear God, please let Mike get hit by a stray bullet.' And then I told her that God answered my prayer in a different way; He gave me the strength to get out of the hell of a marriage I was living in."

"Wow, I have never seen you get so angry." Dr. H made a note in her book. "You must have been very strong to go against everyone and break free from someone I would classify as a narcissist. But I am curious, why didn't you try and seek marriage counseling?"

"Unfortunately, he didn't 'believe' in therapy." I made air quotes. "And I *am* angry. But by the end of the marriage, it was too late for therapy anyway. I was already mentally gone from the marriage. I mean, I was a great wife and a good mother, and I did everything he asked of me. There would be times when I would go meet my girlfriends for lunch or play Bunco or whatever, and he would decide he didn't want me to go at the last minute. When I went anyway, well, I paid dearly for those times. He never hit me, but he would mentally and emotionally abuse me by locking me out of the house or going for days without talking to me. I don't know what he expected to gain by treating me in that manner; all it did was make me end up hating him for the way he treated me.

"He would say: 'It's not right for you to want to leave your kids and go out with your friends. It's just not right.' One Mother's Day, my cousin Terry and her mother, my mother's sister, Aunt Gail, invited my mother and me to meet them in Atlanta to celebrate Mother's Day. So I picked up my mother and drove to whatever restaurant Terry had chosen and we all had a nice lunch; well, they did. I was so nervous and ready for the meal to be over, anxious if you will. I knew what would be waiting for me when I came home. And sure enough, after I had dropped off Mother, he was waiting for me at our door. He had put the kids upstairs with a movie, and he began to ask me, over and over, 'What kind of mother leaves her children on Mother's Day?'

"He would have me questioning myself and doubting everything. I was so accustomed to asking permission for everyday things, I didn't even realize it until I was out of the marriage.

"Terry, the one who is more like a sister to me and tried to talk me into staying, finally saw through Mike's campaign. She reminded me of the time they were in town from Nashville and she and I went to the grocery store. Apparently, we were gone longer than Mike thought was necessary, and he actually showed up at the store to see if we were there."

"Do you think your children ever felt any of this tension?" she asked.

"They were so young, and I tried to hide it from them, so I really don't think they knew."

"So how is it you were vindicated?"

"Oh, right, that's where I began." I took a beat. "After I left Bill, I 'escaped' and went to live with Lydia in her apartment in Atlanta. She was in college at Oglethorpe University in Brookhaven, and I didn't want to go to my parents, who lived in the same country club neighborhood as Bill, or to my sister Kim, who was close by. So Caroline went to stay with her dad, Mike, for the summer, as she was supposed to, and I went to live with Lydia in Atlanta. I know this sounds so fucked up."

"Isn't that why you are here?" Dr. H smiled.

"Yes, I always seem to drift off track, don't I?" I smiled at her and continued. "So I had been living with Lydia for six months, this was 2010. She turned 21 on December 5, my divorce from Bill was final on December 21. She went out of town with her dad the weekend before Christmas. I know it sounds confusing, but just follow the math.

"She and I were sitting in the apartment the night before she left for the weekend with her dad, and she asked me point blank: 'Mom, you've never told me what happened with you and Dad, why you got divorced.' And I looked at her and agreed, so I decided to tell her the truth. She was 21 and finally asking. I explained to her how her dad was so pathologically jealous of me that he treated me as if every time I walked out the door I was going to be with someone else. When I was pregnant with her, he had me cowering in the corner of the kitchen, sobbing with tears pooling in my hands, telling me I had to quit my job with Turner Broadcasting. That's another story. . ."

"Focus," the doctor said.

"I told her about the emotional abuse, the accusations, the tracking me down at the grocery store. How he would punish me if I didn't stay home. How I wasn't 'allowed' to go to lunch or do things with friends or get a babysitter during the day. I told her everything, and she simply said, 'I understand.'

"I wasn't sure if I had done the right thing confiding in my 21-year-old daughter about how horrible her father had been to me, how he treated me, and how destructive he was to my psyche.

"But when she came home from Christmas weekend with her dad and her sister and half-siblings, she rushed into our home. She was so excited when she told me point blank that I wouldn't believe what happened.

"She and Mike ended up driving up to the North Georgia mountains later than everyone else the Friday they left town. Lydia said, during the entire two hours of the car ride, her dad opened up to her about the mental abuse he inflicted on me during our marriage. And everything I had told her, every incident, he told her the same story. He even went so far as to tell her that when I was out to lunch with my girlfriends, that he would come home from the office, go into my closet, and look at my clothes to try to figure out what I wore that day. This was something I didn't realize was happening; it was just insane.

"I couldn't believe he confessed to her, on his own, and that he told her he took one hundred percent of the blame for the end or our marriage."

"That must have made you feel good," she stated.

"In a way, it did. Unfortunately, it only goes to show you how much of a monster he was," I said. "I kept telling my mother how abusive he was, but she didn't see it. I tried to hide all the emotional and mental abuse from my family and friends. But that worked against me; because when I was tired and had enough of the abuse and was finally ready to leave, no one knew about the abuse, about the damage he caused, because I had hidden it so well."

"That's not uncommon in a narcissistic relationship. I would venture to say that is the norm. Not much has been studied in this realm of abuse, and in fact, most narcissists are not diagnosed because they do not see themselves as being abusive. It's a circle of circumstances that are hard to explain unless you have been a victim of narcissistic abuse," she smiled gently with a knowing look in her eyes as if she had experienced this firsthand.

"I often thought that if he had only beaten me, then people would be able to see the bruises, the blood, and the scars. Instead, my scars were carved deep into my mind, hidden so well from the public persona that I projected. Yet they are forever in my psyche, and I wear them as a reminder of how weak I became."

"But you are not weak now," she said. "It's very hard to break free from a narcissist. They keep you in a trauma bond to where you are dependent on their chaos."

I smiled a weak smile and went back to that day when I knew in my heart that I was married to a pathologically jealous man and that one day I would get the nerve to say "no more." Little did I know how hard it would be to break free from a narcissistic bond or that you can never completely cover up an emotional scar, especially one that deep. The pain from the memories of my time with Mike forever stained the fabric of my soul and are a constant reminder that I am broken. You can try to disguise it or try to scrub it clean, but it can never be washed away like your sins. The sadness is isolating, and the thoughts of who I had become to please a man who could never be pleased still haunt me. I covered up my laugh and my light and hid from the world what I was meant to be, and it was still not enough. I fought my way back to myself after I managed to escape from my marriage, but at the end of the day, when the kids were asleep in bed and I was left alone with my thoughts, I realized just how broken I was. Emotional abuse is cruel, for it seeps into your psyche and screams in whispers that only your inner child can hear.

It remains a part of who you are forever.

Chapter 24

Suicide is Painless

Depression comes in many forms, or so I'm told. Mine tends to creep up on me when least expected. It paralyzes my mind with a gentle fog. I lose interest in people and activities, even shopping. It is a soft sort of numbness and is followed by a tremendous need to stay in bed. Perhaps it is the recounting of memories long ago buried, the unexpected remembrance of things past? I blamed these sessions on the depression that had come back to taunt me. After all, had I just been a good little girl, I could have kept these secrets buried and learned to banish the pain in those crevices so long ago created. It's what Mother did . . . and does. She expects us to do the same. To learn to live with whatever life throws our way. She doesn't want to know what happened or acknowledge that our childhood was not perfect. Not to say we didn't have a picture-book childhood. After all, she was and is the perfect mother. But when she found out I was going to therapy, she turned up her nose and told me point blank that she didn't "believe" in therapy. Then she asked me if our childhood was so bad? I told her no, in fact, the reason I had been able to hide my inner self for so long was because she was the most loving and giving and caring mother. So beautiful yet so strong, which to me is a rather cruel combination.

Who was it that said April is the cruelest month? T.S. Eliot? I disagree. August is the cruelest month, to me. It's the month that Elvis died, and Marilyn Monroe, and, most importantly, my sister Jennifer.

It was August, which meant another anniversary of her death to mark with tears, and laughter, and flowers placed on her grave. Grief is a weary emotion. It hits hard some days when you least expect it, or not at all. It's crippling at first, marked with lethargic time spent in bed; then, gradually, the days are gone and years take the place of counting. After five years, you begin to accept the finality of death because you have no other choice. On some days it was harder to be forthcoming about her suicide than others. This was not one of those days.

"People who claim suicide is the most selfish act a person can perform *really* don't understand the strength it takes to complete the act," I said, beginning the session.

"Are you speaking about your attempt, or your sister's suicide?" Dr. H asked, while she arranged the generic tissue box on the glass-top table in front of me. I looked down at the box of tissues; it bothered me that the putrid olive-green checkered pattern of the box so blatantly didn't match the blue and brown decor of her office.

"I'm talking about Jennifer's suicide. She was the strongest person I knew, and she took extra steps to make sure she couldn't save herself this last time. I think about her overdoses and now wonder if she meant to die, because each time before, there was always someone there to save her. Like Sylvia Plath. The poet tried to commit suicide several times before she succumbed. And each time, someone saved her . . . except that last time, of course."

"So you think Jennifer tried to kill herself more than once?" She scooted the box of tissues closer to me.

"I never did before, but, in hindsight, I do. She first overdosed at the home of the couple we babysat for when she was only 13. I have since learned that the same man who molested me had also fucked her. He messed with her first. I often wondered if she became an addict because of that, but then she was diagnosed with bipolar disorder."

"You know, people who are bipolar have one of the highest risks of suicide, so the fact that your sister took her own life isn't as surprising as I'm sure it felt at the time for you and your family."

Thank you, Dr. Obvious, I thought to myself, as I grabbed the top tissue from the olive-green box. Before the tears could pour down and streak my face, I dabbed quickly at the corners of my eyes. *Why does it bother me that this fucking tissue box does not, in any way, match this office? Damn it. And why did I even bother to wear makeup to these sessions? Oh right, I was raised not to go out of the house without being presentable . . . ever.*

"She researched how to die. Two weeks after her funeral, Mother and I went to her house to see if she had left a note. There was no note, per se, but she had put all of her pictures into a photo album and wrote captions underneath each one—kind of a personal note to each of us. While Mother checked the papers on Jennifer's disorganized desk, I pulled up her search history on the computer. She had searched 'Kurt Cobain' and 'death by hanging.'"

"And she chose the latter, which is actually an unusual choice for a woman," Dr. H said. "Usually women are more prone to pills. Gunshots and hangings leave more of a mess behind. Women are always thinking like caretakers, even until the end. It's in our biology, in our blood. We know all about the messes we're expected to clean up." Dr. H paused, pensive.

It made me wonder about the secrets of her past that maybe she had to sweep under the rug. What kind of messes have been left for her to clean up over time?

"Yes, I read about that too. But you see, Jennifer never succeeded with overdosing. I think she was already way too immune to drugs. Even her tolerance was 'high,' so to speak." It was at this point that I *finally* got a smiling reaction from Dr. H in response to my penchant for puns. "She tried them all: pot, cocaine, acid, heroin. It wasn't until she started smoking crack—that was the one she couldn't let go of. So, I guess she chose to hang herself instead.

"I often wondered what her thought process was," I continued. "I mean, she had to have planned it out. She had the rope, the metal bar, which she placed across the opening of the hallway attic she jumped from, and the superglue."

"Superglue?" Dr. H asked, a confused look on her face.

"Yes, superglue. She actually glued her hands together before she jumped. She was so strong, physically and mentally. Much stronger than me or Kim. I guess she was afraid she would be able to use her hands to save herself, so she superglued them together," I stopped for a moment and shuddered at the thought of my strong, big sister gluing her hands together just before her final moments, her last breath.

"I tried to picture her that day in August. She had started her period, of course. She was trying to get off crack and get herself together, so she could get her boys back. Her husband came home from work at lunch to bring her some tampons."

Dr. H stopped me: "Wait, she was still married?"

"Yes, almost twenty-eight years. Jim would never abandon her. He stayed with her until the end. When the courts took the three boys from her, he could have gotten them back if he left Jennifer. But he wouldn't leave her. He said he was afraid that if he left her, she would kill herself. So he stayed. But in the end, it didn't matter. Between the time he'd come home at lunch and came back home again after work, she was gone. He found her hanging in the hallway. Her dog, Hootie, was sitting below her body. She was wearing a blue jean skirt and red T-shirt."

"How do you know what she was wearing?"

"I read the autopsy report, the one that said her hands were superglued together," I said. "I see her all the time in my mind's eye. Going into the hallway. Pulling down the attic stairs by its string. Climbing up. I always wondered if she'd already placed the rope and metal bar up in the attic, and if so, how long had they been there? How long had she planned this? And when was that moment she decided *now* was the time? When did she figure out that her rock bottom had a basement?" I took another tissue from the olive-green box and continued.

"I mean, think of all the steps it took to get her to the moment she jumped out of the attic. It wasn't as simple as swallowing a bunch of pills with a bottle of vodka by your bed; or driving into a garage, pushing a button to close a door, and then simply sitting in a running car."

"Are you saying that your attempt was not real?" Dr. H stopped me and leaned into my personal space. "Based on our conversations during these sessions, it was a real attempt to end your life."

"I'm not saying it wasn't real. I'm just saying it was not planned out like hers. I think all of my past experiences with jealous men flooded into my mind when I drove home from that day of drinking. I was just tired of the same old issues. I was crying so hard when I left the bar. Of course, I'd been drinking margaritas, and tequila can make me crazy, but that's not why I did it. I was tired and had the feeling that nothing was ever going to change. I can't explain why, but for me it was a moment of weakness. I believe, for Jennifer, it was a moment of strength. So, for people to say suicide is a coward's way out, I beg to differ. It's the most courageous act—to be able to let go of a tortured life."

"Do you think her life was always tortured?" she asked.

"Yes. And yet, when I sat down to write her eulogy, all that came back to me were the fun times—the things that made Jennifer, Jennifer."

"Tell me more. I want to know what she was like." She was pushing me further, making me reach under the iceberg, and I shivered at the thought of even more exposure to instances of my vulnerability that I wanted to keep to myself.

"When I sat down to write her eulogy, the words flowed out of me. I started with 'There are three things I want you to remember about my sister: She was intelligent, she was creative, and she was a free spirit.' Then I wrote about all the fun times growing up with Jennifer, all our great adventures that she dreamed or schemed up for us."

"Such as?" asked Dr. H.

"Like the time we had friends visiting from Florida, and we wanted money to go to Bostic's Store for candy, but Mother told us no. *No* never stopped Jennifer, though. I told you about this? She went to the garbage and got a used can and crafted a 'March of Dimes' collection can."

"Ah, yes, the March of Dimes. That was very creative," she said.

"Yes, that was creative. That was Jennifer. But the one story I recalled in my eulogy for Jennifer, that for months after her funeral everyone talked about, was the garbage can man story."

"I'm listening," she smiled.

"Daddy had an old truck, Ford, I think, with two handles and step wells on the outside of each door. I guess they were there to help you get up into the bed of the truck. Anyway, I was maybe 5, making Jennifer 6, almost 7 . . . so Kim would have been 2. Kim was in the front of the truck cab between Mother and Daddy; Jennifer and I were in the bed of the truck, going down the highway. Knowing my daddy now and how he drives, I'm sure we were going over the speed limit. I don't remember where we were headed, but it didn't matter; we never got there. I was singing a song when Jennifer scooted over to me and asked me if I wanted to play a game. Of course, I said, 'Sure. What game?' She answered, 'garbage can man' and proceeded to explain the game to me."

"Oh, I think I see where this is going," she piped in with a curious smile.

"Well, I didn't. Jennifer explained that it was a simple game to play. We were to grab onto the handle and step out of the truck and down onto the step well as we held on tight—just like the garbage men who came to our neighborhood each week. Best of all, I got to go first! So I held onto the rubber-coated chain handle, climbed out of the truck and stood on the step well as we were riding down the highway, still holding on to the handle. The truck had a long side view mirror, and I remember the look on Daddy's face when he looked over in the mirror and saw me on the outside of the truck. When I saw his face looking at me in the mirror, I removed one of my hands and waved to him. The next thing I knew, we were stopped on the side of the road and he was hugging me tight, asking me what in the world was I doing."

"Playing garbage can man!" Dr. H said emphatically, not really asking a question.

"Playing garbage can man," I smiled. "And that's the story *everyone* remembers."

"I can see why," she said.

"They remembered that story and they remembered how I ended her eulogy. I circled back to the beginning and said that Jennifer's genius was too much for one person to handle. That she couldn't fit into this world the way it was expected of her. Then I said that she gave each one of her three boys one of her talents. Luke received her intelligence, Robert her creativity, and Ryan her spirit."

I allowed my tears to flow freely and reached down to pick up a tissue, once again, from the olive-green checkered box that would never belong anywhere in this room, because, like Jennifer, it didn't fit in. It would never fit in, and it would remain out of place until its contents were empty and its shell discarded.

Chapter 25
Chapter and Verse

"I almost threw these away," I said to Dr. H as I handed her the plain tattered manila envelope.

Searching her crowded desk, she put on her glasses and took out the contents from the well-worn envelope. Her glasses had bright red rims with leopard-patterned arms. It hit me why some people called them "spectacles." *Such an odd style choice for her*, I thought. I tried to imagine what she must be like out of her office, what I had come to call my sanctuary. She was extremely attractive, though she hid it well. But her choice in clothes was worse than my choice in men. She was dressed in a uniform of drabness—a navy pantsuit with a brown and blue swirl-print blouse and sensible brown shoes. In fact, she actually matched her office decor, unlike the olive-green box of tissues that had finally been discarded.

Fashion, I know well; it was my career choice from the beginning, a young girl who would dress Barbie for dates with Ken. Ironically enough, that day I was wearing my favorite bracelet from a New York designer. The bracelet's black resin with large cursive cream writing states: *Fashion can be bought. Style one must possess.* My other favorite bracelet, which I wear every time I wear this particular one, was in the car. I took it off before coming into the office since it seemed inappropriate for a doctor's appointment. It is wider than the one I was wearing; cream resin with black writing that says: *Vodka martini, shaken not stirred.*

She took her time reading the mound of papers before her. I adjusted the hem of my black and cream striped Marc Jacobs shirtdress, as my mind aimlessly wandered until her soft voice broke the silence.

"These are all Bible verses dealing with the sins of taking one's own life," she stated, while looking up over the rim of her glasses. "What do they mean?"

"They mean nothing to me and everything," I said flatly. "They were sent to me by an acquaintance of Jean, one of my oldest and dearest friends, a sorority sister, shortly after Jennifer died. They were coworkers. I met the sender only a few times; she'd come when Jean and I would meet for drinks or shopping. I did not know her well, but the "Southern Baptist" in this person felt compelled to compile all the verses in the Bible about suicide being a sin—and send them to me. Jean was very apologetic when she found out what her coworker had sent in the envelope. She would have never given this person my address had she known what she was going to be sending. Needless to say, the envelope did not contain a sympathy card."

Silence fell for a brief moment throughout the room and lingered like an empty promise thrown out to a casual friend.

"Unfortunately, she wasn't the only one compelled to speak out against Jennifer's choice to die," I continued. "The ministers from our church did so as well. Mother asked me to contact the former minister from our childhood church and our former youth minister to perform Jennifer's service. So I did. Of course, they'd already heard the news. It seems like tragic gossip traveled faster than run-of-the-mill gossip," I said with a slightly sad smile as I waxed on about the gossip that surrounded the death of my sister.

"Anyway, I was a bit stunned when they told me they would have to get back to me on whether or not they would conduct her service. After all, as

Mother reminded me when she chose them, these were the leaders of our church and knew us better than anyone. These God-fearing men were the ones who baptized us, married us, and led us out of temptation. Imagine my surprise when I got the call that they were on the fence about presiding over Jennifer's service because they didn't *agree* with the way she died. What the fuck does that have to do with conducting a funeral? I mean, who 'agrees' with the way anyone dies? I was dumbfounded. I called Kim and told her what happened. She called them both and told them they didn't have to do the service is they felt that way. She was so angry. I was lying in bed consumed with grief when the youth minister called me the next day to tell me that they had decided to go ahead and preach at her funeral because our parents were such pillars of the community and the church."

"Did you let your parents know about their hesitation?" she asked.

"No, but I wish I had. I didn't want to hurt my parents any more than they already had been. They were shattered, numb, and in shock. In hindsight, I should have told the ministers not to worry about it, especially since they did a lackluster job, and Mother was so disappointed. They only read from the Bible. No memories recounted; no peaceful, comforting words. It was as if they were hired by the funeral home to conduct the service for some unknown person who committed her final sin. If I hadn't written the eulogy for her, no kind words would have been spoken," I said. "But in a strange way, I am thankful for all the cruel words and whispers about her death."

"Why is that?" She seemed surprised.

"Because I never would've had my dream." I glanced up to the ceiling, while I remembered the night I cried out to God for answers. "It was so powerful and real. My first out-of-body experience, and it brought me comfort, peace, and closure."

"You know our time is up, and you're just now telling me about this dream?"

"It's called burying the lede," I smiled.

Then I thought about Jennifer and the judgment and all the harsh words whispered by people who never knew her, who would never know her the way I did. I was lucky that we were eighteen months apart and I got to know her before her illness took over—before the self-medicating, the wild impulses, the bouts of uncontrolled anger. This was not the funny, energetic, creative person I knew. But I could always find that little girl in her eyes, and I never gave up on her. And she, in turn, never gave up on me.

I gathered my worn envelope full of someone else's issues, put on my Chanel sunglasses, the ones Bill had bought me in Paris, and headed outside to greet the warmth of the Southern sun.

Chapter 26
Soul Sisters

My note this session was simple. I'd written it on my ivory stationery with the LTR monogram that was a gift one Christmas from Mother. She always gave me stationery on which to write my thank you notes, as every proper Southern girl was raised to do. My MR. AND MRS. WILLIAM JOHN TUSH, III engraved notes from Tiffany & Co. were now long out of date, but then again, so was my LTR monogram. *The next time Mother asks me what I want for Christmas*, I thought, *I should tell her I want plain, white stationery, engraved only with an L.*

Though my note was quite simple, it still brought me comfort. It was the childhood prayer Mother and Daddy said to us each night as we knelt down on the floor with our hands folded before us in preparation for bed. The words now took on a whole new meaning.

Now I lay me down to sleep,
I pray the Lord my soul to keep.
If I should die before I wake,
I pray the Lord my soul to take.

"I haven't thought about my dream in quite a while, but ever since I left your office, it's all I can think about," I began. It had only been two weeks since our last session, but somehow, it seemed longer. Maybe it was because I was ready to tell her about my experience, my dream of Jennifer. Finally, I found myself crawling out of the dark cavern into which I had fallen so many years before.

"I haven't shared my experience with many people, other than close friends and family, because it's a very personal story and, quite frankly, I was awakened by the realization that I had been held hostage in the Southern Baptist religious mantra of hell, fire, and brimstone for most of my life. But now I realize that not many people believe in an afterlife, as we were taught when we were children."

"It's all subjective. And the studies I've read on the subject of an afterlife all reflect on the individual and how they react to the situation," she said. "I'm curious to hear about your experience."

I paused to take a deep breath, exhaled my fears, and began.

"After Jennifer died, I would literally cry myself to sleep each night, and my tears would wake me up each morning. I had to make myself get up to get the girls ready and out of the house for school, then I would go back to bed and fall asleep surrounded by my ivory silk sheets and custom Robert Allen cotton duvet made especially for the Eagle's Landing house. Its blush-colored bedroom became a sort of sacred refuge for my grief.

"I would close my eyes and picture Jennifer the last time I saw her in the Edgewood house. The same house we grew up in; the house that Mother and Daddy gave to her in yet another attempt to save her. We were always trying to save her."

I paused when I felt the tears begin to fall upon my cheek, but I was silently crying, thinking: *Now, the house appeared to be a reflection of its owner—tired and worn and desperate for someone to take it over, to make it whole again.*

"I should have done more to help her. She found my house for me, you know? The one in the country club. She called me when Bill and I were in New York and told me she had the perfect house for me. It was this jewelry box of a house, with marble floors, antique chandeliers, and lots of light—and that enormous master bedroom with French doors and a marble bathroom with a canopied bathtub. Our blush bedroom. She said, 'Lisa, this is *your* house. It's like it was made for you.' And she was right. It *was* perfect for me."

Why didn't I give her silk sheets to sleep on, or have a custom duvet made for her bed? They meant nothing to me now. The luxuries I had designed and made in New York are just things I wrapped myself in while grieving for my sister.

"I found myself a prisoner in my perfect house, where I would set my alarm so I could be up when the girls would arrive home in the afternoon from school. I was barely existing; I thought I was hiding my grief, but I was only fooling myself. My grief was so great that my youngest daughter's pediatrician told me that it was causing my daughter to be sick. Her doctor told me I had to get out of bed and start living. She's the one who suggested I go talk to someone. No—you're not my first," I laughed a little as I said this.

"After Carrie's doctor told me I really needed to deal with my grief, I went to see Angie. She was a counselor in the neighborhood, the daughter of an acquaintance, and had the sweetest spirit.

"She tried to get me to go beneath the surface, just like the book she gave me suggested. She was the first to bring up the iceberg metaphor, imploring me to talk about all the reasons I was sad, to dive down deep underneath. But I wasn't willing or able to back then. So, I just stopped going to see her.

"It was a very dark time for me, my parents, and my younger sister, Kim. What was so unbelievable to me was that, in my darkest moments, I had so many instances of people telling me that Jennifer's soul was condemned to hell for taking her own life. For the first time in my life, I started to doubt my faith. Jennifer was a good person—damaged, but good. What's the quote by Charles Bukowski? 'Some people never go crazy. What truly horrible lives they must lead.'

"That sums up the people who judged Jennifer. She tried to find her normal; her mind was anything but. She was a brilliant artist and infinitely creative, and in the end, I do believe she went mad. I think the final straw that broke me was the Bible verses I received after her death. That's what really sent me over the edge."

I paused and pondered about Jennifer's life as an addict. She became addicted to addiction, caught up in a vicious cycle. Like most mentally ill people, she started to self-medicate at a young age. She had tried every drug available and was always able to quit when she had to. But crack cocaine finally got to her. It was the one thing she did that actually made her feel normal. *How do you ask someone to stop something that gave them peace, that made them feel normal?*

"When we were little, our parents used to have parties in our downstairs playroom. We had a huge built-in bar that housed our toys—Barbies, dolls, dress-up clothes for me, toy guns and every kind of ball for Jennifer and Kim. The floor was tiled in that 1960s Formica swirl of cream and green, and we would ride our trikes inside when it was too wet to go out to play. We thought it was huge, but then again, we were only 3, 6, and 8 years old. On the Saturdays of a party, we would take all our toys and put them in the garage. Then, instead of games, dolls, and puzzles, our built-in toy chest would become a bar to house beer, wine, and liquor. Mother would have Daddy take the clear light bulbs from the chandelier and replace them with red ones. Our bike path became the dance floor.

"We would be fed the ubiquitous Swanson's chicken pot pies, which always alerted us it was date night or party night. We would be bathed and put in bed before the neighbors came. Kim would fall asleep first. But Jennifer and I would stay up and listen to the music and the clinking of glasses. One neighbor, Mrs. Bohannon, would boldly come up the stairs and bring us some cocktail food. Then the next morning, when Mother and Daddy were still asleep, the three of us would go downstairs and survey the damage to our playroom. I didn't know it at the time, but while Kim and I would consume the leftover peanuts and olives, Jennifer would drink the vodka or gin, or whatever liquid was left in the glasses. At the time it seemed innocent, but that's when Jennifer started what we had since referred to as her 'self-medicating' period. From there she moved to cigarettes, then pot, quaaludes, cocaine, acid, and who knows what else."

"You still haven't told me about your dream," Dr. H reminded me.

"I'm getting there. I just wanted you to know that her demons began really early. And it must have been exhausting for her. She was 45 when she died, that's thirty-five years of trying to fix herself. It was maybe three months after her death, and I was still heavily grieving, consumed with the knowledge that she was still suffering, that she was damned to hell. One night, I got down on my knees and knelt beside my bed and folded my hands in prayer like we did when we were little. I prayed to God to send me a sign that she was OK. I literally asked God to let me know Jennifer was in heaven. That's the night she came to me."

I paused and remembered the moment distinctly before continuing.

"It was incredibly real, my dream. Jennifer and I were back in the Edgewood house where we grew up together. The house was on a corner lot lined with trees; my favorite dogwood tree was in full bloom. It was strange because, in my dream, we were older in appearance and not children, but I felt as if we were very young—as if we were on the side of the yard on our swings in our matching outfits." I picture this vivid memory that was captured by Daddy in a photo that now sits by my bed.

"We stepped outside the front door, together, on the porch. I looked into our yard, and all the trees that lined the corner of our lot had ropes hanging down from their massive branches. There were seven thick ropes tied into nooses dangling before my eyes." I paused amidst the memory.

"Jennifer and I stepped out into the yard, and a powerful wind came and swept us both up into the sky—into the heavens. Then I was gently placed back down on the ground, and Jennifer was no longer with me. I looked around and all the ropes, the nooses, were gone from the trees. And for the first time, I felt at peace."

"That's a very powerful dream. It sounds more like an out-of-body experience. What did it say to you?" she asked.

"I knew it was God's answer to my prayer. It was His way of letting me know that Jennifer was up in heaven with him and all the earthly burdens she lived with all those years were gone. Just like the nooses. Then it hit me. God could never condemn to hell someone who has suffered all their life. As a father or mother, even though you are disappointed in your children, you would never want them to suffer for the rest of their lives.

"It was our prayer all along," I said as I repeated the last lines of our childhood prayer, the one I handed to her at the beginning of the session. "If I should die before I wake, I pray the Lord my soul to take."

Chapter 27
Three Can Keep a Secret…

There was no one in the waiting room when I arrived for my appointment, which was a bit unusual for a Friday afternoon. The usual suspects I'd come to notice were glaringly absent: The 'tween girl who I was sure was a cutter; the twenty-something boy who was transitioning into a woman; the couple who were either in marriage counseling or grief therapy—or perhaps it's the same thing? All have shared this space. All were experts in the awkward glances and half acknowledgements that seem to suggest we are all fucked up in some way or another. I wondered what they thought of me? The forty-something woman who is always overdressed?

Dr. H opened her door and ushered me into the office. Perhaps she was anxious to get started on our session? I wondered if she'd been waiting to hear the story I kept promising to tell, the one where Bill and I split? She was wearing a new floral dress and hot pink shoes. I was in a black cotton halter dress with an open back and gladiator sandals. We could've been going out for cocktails if we weren't on doctor-patient terms.

I took my seat across from her. She had a new chair, white leather with chrome. She stood out in her brightly colored floral dress like multicolored roses on a white baby grand piano. She seemed different, happy. I wondered if she had met someone, for she had that inner glow of a new relationship, which was ironic since all I talk to her about is doomed romances and tragic endings.

"I always know when a relationship is over for me, I just never know exactly when I'm going to leave." I said matter-of-factly, and for some reason, again, I was reminded of the words of Benjamin Franklin: "Three may keep a secret, if two of them are dead."

"Well, when it came to the end of me and Bill, it was August 8, 2009."

"Why is that date so precise, when the others haven't been?" she wondered out loud.

"It was the day of his son's wedding," I told her and then went back in my mind to the events leading up to that fateful date.

"Bill had started to drink more and more since he had a heart issue the previous year. The health incident left him with a pacemaker he didn't need and a personality change no one knew how to deal with. He started to drink vodka regularly, when before he just drank Sam Adams and red wine. He became darker and darker, and his depression revealed itself in his treatment of me, my daughters, and my family.

"He would complain about having to go to Mother and Daddy's home for holidays or birthdays, and frankly, no one wanted him to come. I would tell him he didn't have to come, and we would leave him at home. Unfortunately, he would stew about it and show up anyway. Everyone would be relieved when the girls and I would arrive without Bill in tow; then they couldn't hide their disappointment when he would waltz in, flask of vodka in hand, and proceed to cut down everything from the casseroles to the kids."

"How long did this go on?" she asked.

"From May 2008 until the day I walked out of the house in June 2010."

"That's a long time to put up with any kind of abuse," she noted, again.

"I know," I responded. "Like I said, I have a habit of staying in a relation-ship too long before I actually leave."

"But if it started in May 2008 and you say you knew in August 2009, then why did you hang in almost a year longer?"

"Certain circumstances always kept getting in the way."

"Please, tell me." She put her pen down and stared at me as if to say, *you have my full attention.*

"For over a year, I put up with his slide into darkness, depression—whatever you want to call it. We didn't have sex for a lot of reasons, but mainly because he was always too drunk, or I was mad and upset. He started to pick on me and the girls. He would complain about everything and everyone. His biggest complaint centered around Caroline. She had turned 16 and started driving, so she was gone most of the time. Like most 16-year-olds with freedom, she started to eat out at fast food places and, therefore, started to gain weight.

"Well Bill, who used to be on TV, couldn't stand the fact that she was gaining weight. He would drop hints to her all the time; make snide remarks; praise Lydia for how small she had gotten while away in college. But worst of all, whenever Caroline came into a room, he would make the beeping sound that a large truck makes to let you know they are backing up."

"That's so cruel," she commented.

"My love for him gradually turned into despising him, and then on August 8, 2009—to pure hatred."

"I'm listening," she said.

"He was continually harping on about Caroline's weight; he embarrassed her in front of her friends so much that they stopped coming around. He would go through the groceries when I came home from the store and take out the things we were 'not allowed' to have. He wouldn't let her go out to eat with us; he basically isolated her in her room. Even Penny, our dog, was afraid of him. Penny started to stay with Caroline in her room.

"Eventually, I think he realized I started to pull away emotionally and physically, so he was becoming more and more possessive. He was frustrated because we were not having sex, and he was used to getting it whenever he wanted it up until then.

"He was emceeing the Southeast Emmy Awards; a gig that our business partner Dave got for him. In fact, Bill's drinking had gotten so bad that I didn't want him out in public, but he sobered up for this one event. It was in June 2009, two months before that fateful night, and the SE Emmys were held in a hotel in Buckhead. Dave was a former stand-up comic turned comedy writer. We met him when we pitched TBS about a show for Bill. They hired Bill and me to do a web-based series, and Dave was the head writer/producer on the show. He was very talented at highbrow comedy.

"Anyway, Dave pitched Bill to host the SE Emmys, and that's how Bill found himself employed, albeit briefly. Dave was such a fan of Bill's he tried almost as hard to find him work as I did. Bill retired in 2002, just after 9/11. He took off two years in compliance with his noncompete with CNN, and by the time he was ready to go back to work, he couldn't find anything 'good' enough. I pitched so many shows to so many producers for too many years. From 2003 until we met Dave in 2007, it was me pitching and pushing him. We had such an incredible life in New York; I was so happy being his wife and attending all the fun events on his arm. But in the end, I lost a lot of respect for him. Adam, his producer at CNN, who was his biggest fan, also tried to help by booking him shows, but Bill wouldn't lift a finger to help me; he sat around the house waiting for the next big opportunity to come knocking at the door.

"I gave up trying, but not Dave. I, of course, was there at the event to protect him as his publicist. The Emmy people rented a hotel suite for us to use after the show. He did the show, we went to the after party, and then went back to the suite, where my dear friend Kerri was waiting for us.

"I didn't really think about why she wanted to meet us after for a drink, but it turns out she had other things in mind. I don't think she realized just how broken Bill and I were and that we hadn't been together in a while. Her showing up was probably the only reason I ended up having sex with Bill that night."

"How did it start?" she asked. "I mean who initiated the session?" I laughed a little at her question.

"She started it," I told her. But it started many years before when we were both "hostage housewives" living in Fayetteville.

"So the pursuit was of you?' Dr. H asked.

"Yes," I answered. "It was always about me. When we lived in Fayetteville, we had a mothers' group that would meet every Tuesday and Thursday for breakfast at the local Chick-fil-A. There were about twelve of us total, with the majority of us showing up each time was the norm." I took a sip of my LaCroix. Lemon-flavored, sans wine.

"We all had kids the same age, preschoolers, and we would take them to Mother's Morning Out at the Methodist Church on the square at nine a.m., then head for breakfast. We would complain about our husbands, eat our chicken biscuits, and drink our coffee, then head back to pick the kids up by noon. It was our therapy time, and we never missed a breakfast if we could help it."

"It is good to have close girlfriends when your children are young and you have a lot in common?"

At first, I thought this was a statement, but she ended it with a question in her voice.

"Well, turns out some of us got *very close*." I let this statement linger.

"I feel as if we have another story about to unfold," she said.

"Well, you asked about Kerri and how it got started."

"Yes, but I was talking about the threesome with Bill."

"I realize that, but once I begin to think about how it started, I realize it actually began ten years before, when the six of us close friends from Fayetteville went on a fateful trip to celebrate a birthday. Initially, I wasn't 'allowed' to go since it involved a private plane and a private boat, and Mike was not about to sanction that kind of dream trip. But I defied him and went anyway. After all, it was my best friend's birthday, and her husband had arranged for the six of us to go on his friend's private plane to Stuart, Florida, where he kept his boat."

"How were the six of you going to be staying on a boat?" She seemed confused.

"Well, technically, it was a yacht that slept six. They had their own captain to take us out on the water. Mike was so furious when I called him, just as I was getting on the plane, to tell him the girls were with my mother, who agreed to watch them while I was gone." I smiled when I remembered this tidbit.

"So we all go to Tara Field, get on the plane, and fly down to Florida. It was Kerri, Chris, Taylor, Samantha, me, and Mandy, the birthday girl."

"We did tequila body shots on the way down, and by the time we landed we went directly to the boat, put on our bathing suits, and had the captain take us out for a ride. We danced, drank champagne, and went topless while we laid out. Funny, we kept noticing all these boats cruising by . . . seems word got out that the boat had mermaids on its front."

She didn't say a word.

"Looking back, that trip was a turning point for all of us. I knew I was going to be in trouble; that was a given. Turns out, so were Kerri and Samantha. Taylor and Chris were okay, as was Mandy.

But after that trip, four of the six of us would be divorced within two years. I was first, and then Kerri . . . then Chris, I think."

"What happened on that trip?" She was curious, and it showed.

"What didn't happen?" I was sarcastic and shouldn't have been.

"First of all, it turns out that Kerri and her husband had been enjoying the company of Samantha without her husband. Samantha was the daughter of a Baptist minister from South Georgia. Her husband, whose name I can't recall now—in fact, I'm not sure I ever knew it—was big into the church. They had three little kids, and I think Samantha wanted to be in our group so badly she would do anything. She was the youngest of us by ten years; we were in our early thirties. She was maybe 24? It was that weekend when we all found out about the three-way and the affair."

"How did it come up?" Dr. H was taking furious notes, so much so that I wondered if I would turn out to be a subject in a book.

"Mandy and I, the tame ones on that trip, slept upstairs while the other four took the master and bunks down below. They all had their own little party while Mandy and I slept off our champagne and suntans."

"What kind of party?"

"The kind one has when one first goes off to college. You know, of an experimental nature," I felt as if I had to paint the picture for her. I sighed. "They engaged in group sex, Doctor. I think there was a hairbrush involved. And that's how the Kerri-Samantha thing came to light."

"And you?" She tried not to act shocked by what I had described.

"I was the good girl." I sighed again. "When we went out to dinner that night, the other girls were flirting with the boat captains, who all lived either on the boats in the yacht club or nearby. Apparently, we were the talk of the club, and they wanted to meet us."

"But you didn't participate?"

"No, not the least bit interested. Mandy and I went back to the boat and went to sleep alone while the others partied with the boat captains."

"So your husband's fears were unfounded?"

"I never cheated on him," I responded, not offended. "Besides, if I were going to cheat on him, it would have been with the boat's owner, not its captain."

"That's very elitist. I am surprised to hear you say it like that," she smiled while pretending to scold me.

"You made a joke," I smiled back. "Yes, very 'trophy wife' of me."

"It was that weekend that we all found out about Kerri and Tim and Samantha and their extramarital activities. It was also when I found out that Kerri's husband asked her to ask me to join them. I'm not sure if she wanted me or it was his idea, but she first broached the subject on that fateful trip."

"And did you?"

"With Tim, um, no. He was such an uptight control freak, blazing hair, cute but so not my type. I mean, I used to get hit on and approached by my friends' husbands all the time, but never would I act on it. I was as loyal to my friends as I was to my husbands. You can see where that has gotten me." I smirked. "In the end, it was Kerri who wanted *me*, and she made a pass when I finally divorced Mike."

"What does that mean?" she asked. *Gosh, she is clueless*, I thought.

"It means that she kissed me one night when we both went out dancing after our divorces."

"So she got divorced too?"

"Yes, she was next after me." I chuckled when I thought about it. "Her husband blamed me for their divorce. He told her just because I got one didn't mean she had to. Especially because she divorced him after she found out he was having a 'twosome' with Samantha without her. Men can be so dumb.

"My mother always told me that men were so stupid. That if they only knew how easy it was to please a woman, how simple it was. They are clueless when it comes to pleasing a woman."

"Yes, you have mentioned this theory before. Do you think it's in general or for trophy wives?"

"Definitely in general. I mean, at least the guys who go after trophy wives know how to wine, dine, and make a woman feel like she's someone worth attaining."

"So, a trophy in all respects?"

She is beginning to understand, I thought.

"Yes, they go after you so aggressively, then once you are theirs, they put you on a shelf and mark you off their list. At least that's how I see it. Anyway, where was I? Oh, yes, me and Kerri and Bill."

"Yes, how did this come about?"

"It wasn't planned. The only thing that was planned was that Kerri was going to join us after the event for a drink. So she came up to our suite, and I fixed her something; I don't remember what. In hindsight, I think she came to the hotel that evening specifically for a threesome. So there I am, sitting on the couch with her and Bill is in the chair next to me. Next thing I know, she gets on the floor in front of Bill and starts to suck his very long fingers. Then at the same time, she starts to massage my leg. Well, we both knew what she wanted; I think we had teased about it for years. And, like I told you, she and her ex-husband were known to have had threesomes . . . so it just happened."

"How does it 'just happen'?" She wanted specifics.

"Neither Bill nor I saw it coming, but we just went with it. She started kissing Bill and reaching out to me, so we all got up and made our way into the bedroom. Then she kissed him and fondled me. I kissed her and we fell into bed. Funny thing is and it's true, I heard something from my director friend. . ."

"What's that?"

"He told me the problem with a threesome is it inevitably turns into a twosome, and usually it's the guy who gets pushed out and has to settle for watching instead."

"I really don't think I can comment on this on any level," Dr. H confessed.

"Well, I'm not a threesome expert either, but I would say, from my one experience, that it is true."

"Then I will take your word on that," she said and looked at her watch.

"I know," I said. "Time's almost up and I haven't gotten to August 8th. I'll wrap up the Emmys evening story and save the rest for next time."

"If I didn't have an appointment after you, I would ask you to stay and finish. I think we are making quite a bit of interesting progress here." She smiled as if to say, *you've come a long way with therapy.*

I wrapped up the conversation, for I, too, have an "appointment" after our session.

"I won't go into details, but it was the most honest and loving and gentle expression of desire I had ever experienced. When it was over, she got up and left the two of us in the bedroom as she made her way to the living area, dressed and left. Bill joined me in bed, but I was left with the memory of her as he made love to me, which turned out to be for the very last time."

Chapter 28
Hot August Night

Ever since I was a little girl, I was consciously aware of people not liking me. Perhaps it started with my big sister, Jennifer, and manifested quite clearly with my little sister, Kim. This was a hard pill to swallow since our entire lives we were told that we must obey all the rules so that people will think the best of us. We must not make waves, or break traditions, or cause any scene to draw attention away from the fact that we were proper girls from the South. It was easy for my mother; she was perfect. Perfectly groomed, perfectly mannered, perfectly gorgeous. Yet people did not like her; well, women did not like her.

Unfortunately for her, and well out of her control, we three girls also possessed the DNA of our father. He was quite handsome and had an extremely funny dry sense of humor that was a signature of his maternal Roe side of the family. He did have a bit of an adventurous wild streak that he inherited naturally from his father's side of the family. It was well known that the Rayner girls, his aunts in Alpharetta, were "wild" and had a bad reputation. So bad that my grandmother, Kate, moved her children from the homeplace in Alpharetta to Sandy Springs, then Ben Hill . . . as far away from the three Rayner girls as she could get them. She didn't allow her children much access to those aunts and uncles. She tried to protect them from the "wildness" that apparently ran rampant in the small towns of Alpharetta and Roswell in north Fulton County. But you can try and run away from your DNA for only so long. And try as we may, we could not hide our "wild" side, Baptist upbringing or not.

"You don't think any differently of me, do you?" I said as I sat down on the couch. It's such my Southern Baptist upbringing to even ask, I realized, but it's how I am wired. Then I think, *No wonder Christians do not go to confession; we would never be able to look the preacher in the eye during Wednesday night Bible study if we had to confess our sins each week.*

"You know I am not here to judge you," she said. "Only to listen."

I nodded my head but still couldn't shake the feeling that she didn't know what to make of me or of my past. It had been almost a year to the day that I began my therapy. I had graduated to once-a-month meetings, which was a milestone for me. But this being our almost one-year anniversary, I had come back for an extra session. Call it a gift to myself, for I am known to celebrate anniversaries in big ways.

I waited for her to speak this time.

"When you left last week, you had a very specific date in mind; I'd like to start with August 8 and see if we can keep on track today."

"Yes," I said. "Saturday, August 8, 2009. That was the date of Bill's only child's wedding. J had met his fiancé while working at a large craft store. He was always telling Bill that he was going to be 'bigger' than Bill was on TV, and he ended up working in a craft store so he could build models of the World Trade Center buildings, which he became unusually obsessed with after 9/11.

"He was a conflicted boy—partly because he was poisoned against Bill by his mother. Yet he was so proud of his dad. Why parents do that to their children I will never understand. As much as I despised the girls' father, I never once said anything bad against him to them." I saw the look she was giving me, which said she understood.

"I know how hard it is to want to 'tell' your side of the story to your children. But you have to remember that they are just that, children. And they do not hold the 'adult' mentality to process the facts. So good for you for resisting the urge to tell them. It is very difficult, especially when the other party is not playing by the same rules." She offered this to me in a way that said, *I have been there too.* "Please, continue."

"So, it is six weeks after the threesome, and Bill has grown angry with my lack of affection toward him. My 'trophy wifeness' seems to be wearing off on him. Maybe I've been marked off and put up on a shelf? I, on the other hand, have grown weary of his constant negativity, complaining, and meanness to my children, my family, and my friends. I literally have lost all respect for him, and that is a terrible thing to lose in any relationship. Bill decided he didn't want to attend his son's wedding, but I told him he had to go and that I would go with him. We had yet to meet his fiancé or be asked to be involved in the wedding festivities, except for the lone invitation to the event.

"The bride was from a small town just off Interstate 20 on the way to Augusta, about forty-five minutes east from Atlanta. The wedding would take place in the town's Conyers Recreation Center, which I learned later was because the bride and her sisters were big into clogging, and apparently, clogging is allowed in the Conyers rec center. Do you know what clogging is, Doctor?"

"Yes, it's a form of folk dance," she smiled then added, "I, too, am from the South."

"'Folk dancing' is a kind way of putting it. It's like country tap dancing," I laughed. "Anyway, for months I had been putting up with Bill and all his cruelty to my daughter over her weight. When we arrived at the venue, I was somewhat pleased to see the bride was a rather large girl and each sister or bridesmaid was larger than the next. I expected Bill to say something like, 'If your sisters ankles look like that then don't choose a tea-length dress.'

"But then, I guess it is harder to clog in a long gown," I added.

"I will give you that one." Dr. H smiled.

"Thank you," I said and continued. "At any rate, I kept waiting for the punchline from Bill—the one-liners about the recreation center or the clogging or the heft of the bride and her maids . . . but *nothing*! He said nothing to make fun of them, nothing derogatory. Not. One. Thing. And to make matters worse, he was nice. Nice to his ex, nice to his former in-laws, nice to the bride's family. Nice! I couldn't believe it. He was Bill Tush again, someone I had not seen in years.

"And the more I thought about it, the madder I got. I thought to myself, 'You mean the old Bill is still in there? You can be nice if you want to; you just choose not to be?' I was furious. I won't even go into the flowers or the food or the music and how terrible they were; after the reception, as I was sitting in the car as we drove off, I waited. Waited for the derogatory comments about the entire affair, the smart-ass, cut-to-the-bone snide observations about the entire day—the complete annihilation of the country clogging in the recreation center ceremony. But none came. Not *one*. After a few minutes of silence, I was in shock and I went off on him about how dare he not say *one* comment about the size of the girls, the craft store décor, the fucking clogging on the Formica dance floor; how he was actually nice to people—all of it. I went completely mental on the car ride home.

"And then a calm came over me. And I knew, that was it. It was over. We were over. I was through. We drove the rest of the way home, and I didn't say another word. When we arrived at the house, I called my friend Deanne who lived nearby, grabbed a bottle of champagne from our stash, and went to stay at her house. We talked about 'August the Eight,' because that was the exact wording on the wedding invitations. And a calm came over me, again."

"What was the calm?" Dr. H leaned in.

"It was the calm of knowing that I didn't have to make things right with him. That my walking on eggshells, my trying to please him by keeping the girls away from him, my catering to his every whim was over. Fuck it. I was through. My marriage ended that day. In my mind, I was free from obligation."

"But in reality, you were still married."

"Yes, but I gave myself permission to let go."

"What happened next?" she asked while making more notes in her black leather notebook.

"The next Saturday we were invited to hear Paul McCartney perform in Piedmont Park. The young girl who once worked at our country club and who now worked in marketing for a nearby luxury hotel invited Bill and me, along with our friends Kelly and Scott, to be their VIP guests for the concert. I had already agreed to go and tried to tell Bill not to come, but he insisted on going and ruining everyone's evening."

"And did he?" she asked.

"Oh yes, of course, he did," I replied. "Kelly and Scott have a limo, which they used to attend all of the Atlanta events, so they picked us up and we were driven to the hotel. Well, actually, I don't think Scott could come, so we ended up inviting another girlfriend, but I can't remember who. I do remember we started off at the VIP suite of the hotel with food and wine. The staff had already gone to the park and reserved the area where we were sitting with blankets. When it came time to go to the concert, we walked the short distance into the park and made our way to the hillside where the hotel had permission to set up. When we got to the area, Bill went nuts. He said it wasn't VIP enough for him and he wanted to go back.

"Well, he was so drunk and needy that he couldn't make it back alone; it looked like a big storm brewing, so Kelly and Bill and I made our way back toward the hotel, leaving our hostess and her other guests on the lawn. The plan was for us to take Bill to the limo, then Kelly and I would go to the restroom, grab a drink, and make our way back to the park for the concert. By the time we made it to the hotel and put Bill in the limo, it began to rain and then the bottom dropped out. So we ended up having to hang out on the hotel's patio, ordering champagne and waiting for the storm to pass."

"So you had to take him back to the limo? He was so high maintenance that he couldn't go by himself?" She looked surprised.

"Oh, yes. He was always accustomed to having a handler, being on TV and getting the star treatment. However, since he was off the air for almost nine years, he became more and more so. He passed out in the limo, and Kelly just told the driver to keep the air on. Bill thought he was going to be taken home, but the driver did what Kelly said and remained parked at the hotel.

"The table next to us on the patio was a group of actors and directors from L.A. who were there to shoot a TV pilot. We ended up talking, and before we knew it, the storm had passed with Bill still passed out in the limo, but so had the concert. We had been drinking with them for three hours and had become fast friends. The director was the son of a famous old Hollywood director, and he and I became engaged in conversation and forgot about everyone else.

"We were talking and drinking champagne, and the next thing I knew, Bill walked up to me on the patio and yelled, 'What the fuck are you doing? I thought I was going to be taken home!' Everyone stopped, dead cold, and looked at me. Bill walked inside the hotel and one of the actors looked at me with such sympathy and said, 'Are you going to let him speak to you like that?'

"Everyone was stunned, and I was too. But my mood turned to embarrassment when the director said, 'She's probably used to it.' And sad to say, I was. That's when I knew."

"Knew what?"

"That I was going to see the director again."

And before the week was over, I would.

Chapter 29
Make a Wish

I find it sad that men will never truly experience the bond that women enjoy when they find that certain circle of friends. I was pondering this as I drove away from another girlfriends' birthday luncheon at the café at Neiman Marcus. I am truly blessed to have amazing women who pick each other up, dust each other off, and say, "Fuck them if they can't take a joke," while handing you a glass of champagne. That's what I have in my crew of beautiful, accomplished, kind, and generous friends. They know of my suffering and each one in her own way has lifted me up and enabled me to become strong. They have supported me and embraced me and shown me that I am not in this alone. I think this has been as much a part of my healing process as my time with Dr. H.

I had a slight spring in my step, one that was missing the same time the previous year. I was wearing a new outfit Mother gave me for my birthday, or rather, gave me the funds to purchase. I don't think she would have chosen what I was wearing—a white, off-the-shoulder Hérve Léger bandage dress with champagne-gold Jimmy Choo strappy sandals. It was, after all, my birthday luncheon. Unfortunately, I didn't have time to change before my four p.m. appointment with Dr. H. Our lunches always seem to last a good four hours, which is why they usually go straight into happy hour somewhere else. But I had to beg away that day so I could make it on time for my therapy.

"I promised myself I wouldn't go to certain places, and yet here, with you, I find that it's an impossible promise to keep," I began.

"I think that's a good thing, don't you?" Dr. H asked. "That is why you are here, remember? It's a safe place to land."

"I keep asking myself why I am here; why I keep coming back." I was honest and open, and finally ready to go explore long-forgotten places and fresh-cut wounds.

"You know you can stop anytime you like. No one is forcing you to come." She smiled that knowing smile that says these sessions have been good for me.

"Aren't you going to ask me about my choice of outfits?" I asked.

She smiled and pulled out a brown paper-wrapped present, which looked like a book. "Happy birthday," she smiled, "I figured you might be dressed for the occasion."

I smiled and took the gift and put it next to my cream YSL clutch. "Thank you," I said as I looked at the gift—a sea-scented candle—and began our session.

"I went back and read the letter I wrote to my 4-year-old self, the one I showed you in the beginning, and I cried."

"I cried when I read it too," she admitted. "But I think it was a big breakthrough."

"Yes, I guess it was. But our last session was too. In fact, I feel that I am ready to continue the conversation and get it all out of my system. To close the chapter on Bill."

"That's a good step," Dr. H said. I thought, *She is proud of me.*

"It's funny, I basically shut the door on him when I walked out of the house that first day of June 2010. But it was the time leading up to the departure that was very painful for me."

"I'm here," she said simply, and I began.

"Let's see, where did I leave off?"

"I believe you were on a hotel patio with newfound friends when your husband came up to you and yelled something foul at you in front of everyone." She was looking at her notes.

"Oh yes, that's right. So, after Bill woke up in the limo and made that scene in front of everyone, Kelly had the driver take him home, and she and I stayed and drank with the film crew. We didn't leave till well after two in the morning. I gave the director my cell phone number and he gave me his card, and by the time I got home I had a text from him.

"I arranged to meet him the next day at his hotel. I told Bill I had to pick something up at Neiman's for a dinner party we were having that night. I prefer Neiman Marcus to Saks; it's like Manolo Blahnik and Christian Louboutin. You are either a Manolos girl or a Louboutins girl, but never both. I'm a Neiman's girl. Except when I lived in New York City, then I was a Saks girl. Anyway, I did go to Neiman's and picked up some cookies from the tearoom, but then I found myself back at the hotel where I had a drink with the director in the lobby. He invited me up to his room, and I went. I was so nervous. I had been married to Bill for more than ten years, and I had never once cheated on him. But here I was in this Hollywood director's suite flirting and skirting around the reason I was there."

"So you went to sleep with him?" she asked.

"I don't know why I went: To punish Bill? To get him out of my mind? Truth is, by the time I sat down on the couch, I knew I couldn't go through with it."

"So what happened?"

"We talked. Shared our love of writing and poetry. He 'showed' me around the room and when he pulled me onto the bed, I couldn't do it. I apologized, adjusted my little black dress, straightened myself up, and left. I didn't think

I would hear from him again because he was married, but we began a texting relationship."

"Married? How long did that last?"

"Well, that was August. Bill and I were invited to go to the Emmys in L.A. that September. When the director found out I was coming into his town, we made arrangements to meet for dinner."

"How did you pull that off?" She sounded more like a friend than a shrink.

"I arranged for Bill to go back home a day before I did; I told him that Rivka, my friend from New York was in town and I wanted to stay and have a 'girls' dinner with her."

"And he did?" She seemed surprised.

"Yes. He tried to stay, but I convinced him it was best for him to leave. It would be the last time we slept in the same bed. After my return to Atlanta, after my tryst with the director in L.A., it was *really* over."

"So you ended up sleeping with the director?"

"Yes. He came to my hotel and picked me up for dinner in what I am sure was a very expensive sports car that I was supposed to be impressed with, but I have no clue when it comes to cars. Anyway, we had a wonderful meal with lots of champagne. We drove back to the hotel with the top down—did I mention it was a convertible? I invited him up, and we went straight to bed. How does the song go—'She didn't even have to pretend she didn't know what for'?"

"And how was it?"

"It was," I pursed my lips as I tried to find the correct word to describe the moment, "*different*. We had been flirting via text, so there was a big buildup. He was overly experienced and enjoyed rough sex. I was not quite prepared, literally, to be flung all around. But as far as a good old-fashioned revenge fuck goes, it was the perfect one."

"*Revenge fuck?*" I didn't think she had ever heard the term.

"Yes, the proverbial and literal, 'Fuck you!'"

"By this time, you could bring yourself to sleep with the director?" she inquired in the matter-of-fact manner expected from a psychologist.

"Yes, I had to pretend to be nice to Bill so I could go to the Emmys. I know that sounds mean, but I needed to get him out of my system. And for me, that's finding someone else."

"A married someone else?" She looked disappointed.

"An unhappily married, lives in another state, never have to see him again, someone else. I know, but it was the transition I needed. You see, I really loved Bill and thought he was my soulmate. I thought we would grow old together. It's hard to give up on someone when you thought they were your whole future. And it's hard to stay with someone who is an egomaniac, abusive, alcoholic jerk. I did what I had to do."

"And then after the Emmys?"

"It was horrible. In my mind, I was already gone, but physically I was still in the house. He did move downstairs to the terrace level in one of the guest suites. I was up in the master bedroom. He would wake up in the morning, burst into my room, and ask, 'How did the princess sleep?' I stayed in my room or went to my mother's or a friend's house, but I was always home when Caroline came home from school. I would never let her be alone with him and his abusive behavior.

"Lydia was in college in Atlanta, so not that far away from the storm. She came home early for Thanksgiving because Caroline had told her that Bill and I were living in different parts of the house, in different bedrooms. Anyway, she surprised us. Bill was on one of his tirades about how it was 'his' house and he should be the one sleeping upstairs, so he threw me out of the master bedroom; that's when I went downstairs to the Palm Springs Suite."

"The Palm Springs Suite?" she asked.

"Oh, yes, we named our guest bedrooms. The Palm Springs Suite was the furniture that came from our place in Palm Springs. The Manhattan Suite, where Bill was living, was our bedroom furniture from his penthouse apartment in New York, hence the names of the rooms.

"Anyway, he went on a tirade and told me to go sleep downstairs, that he was going to take the master bedroom upstairs. I never fought him on anything, not when he was so drunk. I packed my little bag of essentials, and I went downstairs. Well, he followed me down and started yelling, 'Who are you fucking, 'cause I know it's not me? So you must be fucking someone.' I just went into the room and locked the doors, laid on the bed, and cried.

"Shortly after, I hear this faint knock on the door and Lydia's voice; it sounded so soft and small. She said, 'Mom, it's me; open the door.' There she was, standing there in the hallway—crying.

She explained that Caroline had told her about what was going on, and she came home early to talk to us and see if she could help. I don't know how long she had been in the house, but she had heard and seen Bill. She said, 'I'm sorry, Mom. I had no idea it was this bad.'"

"What did you do?" Dr. H handed me a tissue to wipe the tears I didn't realize were falling from my eyes.

"Thank you," I smiled a half-smile. "I gave Lydia a hug and told her I was sorry. That it looked like I had messed up again."

"But you aren't to blame for his drinking. You know that, right?"

"I know. I hated for my girls to have to go through another divorce. I guess that's why I tried to make it work, to give it the old college try."

"So that was November, and you stayed for another six months?"

"I was trying to make it through Christmas. He, of course, came again to my mother and father's house, and like the Grinch he was, he ruined it for everyone. We would always go to my aunt and uncle's lake house in the north Georgia mountains for New Year's, so I went alone without him. Left him to stew. Caroline and Lydia were at their dad's, and I needed a break. Besides, I got to be with my cousin Terry, who is really more like my sister. She and her mother, my favorite aunt, always remind me that I am loved. It was a good weekend for me. Lots of clarity. I was driving back to Atlanta from the lake and had a few appointments to look at places to move. I was planning on renting a condo for Caroline and me near where Lydia went to college.

"That's when Lydia called me to tell me Caroline wasn't doing well. I rushed home and found her in bed having an asthma attack. She kept telling me she was OK, but it was obvious something was wrong. I took her to the doctor. Long story short, she was taken by ambulance to the local hospital with an oxygen level of eighty-five. They worked on her and couldn't get the level up, so we ended up being transported to the children's hospital. By the time we reached the emergency room, her oxygen level had dropped to seventy-three."

"Oh my," she gasped.

"I know. I almost lost her. They worked on her for three hours before admitting her to the ICU. There she spent a week with a code blue sign on her door. Finally, they were able to take her off oxygen, but still couldn't get her levels up, so we ended up in a regular room. She almost died. The doctors told me stress could be a cause and that I needed to take her home and try to have things as normal and calm as possible.

"I spent almost two weeks in the hospital, and Bill came to see her once. My nephew Robert brought him, because he was too drunk to drive himself. I knew I couldn't move her and change schools, it would have been too much stress on her. So I toughed it out in the same house with him longer than I had planned, trying to make the best of it. All the while, I was preparing to leave. I contacted an attorney. I started packing up some things. Bill would stand over me and tell me what I could and could not take during those times. One day he was going to leave; then the next day he was staying and I would have to go. He had been seeing a heart doctor after his pacemaker incident, and I insisted on going with him. This was March. When we got to the office, I admitted to the doctor that Bill was drinking from the time he got up in the morning until he passed out around seven p.m. at night.

"Bill still thinks I conspired with the doctor to put him into rehab, but I didn't. And the doctor knew by his blood pressure and his demeanor that something had to be done or Bill was going to die."

"So you put him in rehab?"

"Yes. He was there for almost a month. I went to see him every day. He hated the food in the place, so I brought him his favorite sandwich, a Cuban, each day for lunch."

"That was kind of you," she said.

"He was still my husband. Funny thing, naive that I was, when I went to pick him up after he was released from rehab, I thought he would be nice." I laughed out loud. "Instead, he was just as mean as before, but sober."

"They call that a dry drunk," she offered.

"Yes, and I found out the hard way what the definition of one was. That was late April. I confided in my newly obtained divorce attorney, a woman whose name now escapes me, about Bill's rants and rages. She advised me to get a voice-activated tape recorder and to tape my conversations with Bill. So I made my way to RadioShack and purchased one; I kept it by my nightstand so I could tape his outbursts. By this time, I was spending most of my days in bed, in hiding.

When I went back to my next appointment, two weeks later, I placed the tape recorder on the conference table and began to play the tapes. After what seemed like an endless amount of verbal abuse, she reached over and pressed stop. Then she looked at me, with her finger still on the recorder, and said, 'I want you to listen to me very carefully. You need to go home and start think-ing about what you want to take from the house. Then you need to figure out a time when he will be gone from the house for a long length of time. Then you need to ask your sister and your friends to come over and help you pack; you need to arrange for a moving service to be there as well. And then you need to leave. Be prepared that what you take with you that day might be the only things you will ever see from that marriage. Do I make myself clear?'

"Oh my," Dr. H gasped. "I take it she thought you were in danger?"

"I was so wrapped up in surviving that I didn't realize that this was what she was saying to me."

"Did you leave immediately?" she asked.

"No, this was . . . early May? I didn't find a time to leave until June. I had to wait for Bill to go someplace for more than a couple of hours. He didn't have a job or many friends other than his drinking buddies at the club. I tried to keep up appearances with my girlfriends by attending the weekly lunches that my friend Mary threw, or attending whatever ball or charity luncheon I could. But it became harder to hide the abuse. I know my friends realized this, they were always there for me, it was I who didn't want to tell them the truth."

"Yes, good friends know instinctively when something is not right," she smiled.

"And I have the best of friends. To this day, I could call on all of them and they would be there for me. And I am talking about all my different groups."

"What do you mean by different groups?" she asked.

"I had my country club friends, my charity circuit friends, my girlfriends' luncheon friends, my college sorority sisters . . . "

"That's quite an impressive number of groups."

"Yes, but they are all dear, good, true friends. I am blessed to have them in my life. And my sister and cousins too."

"So what transpired between April and June?"

"Caroline would be out of school after Memorial Day, the last weekend in May, which was also graduation. She was a junior, but her best friend was graduating."

I guess I had a strange look on my face, for she asked me: "What did you just remember?"

I half laughed.

"Caroline, her friend, and I were in my bathroom getting ready to go to the school when Bill burst in. He looks at the girls and asks them, 'Where are you two going?' They answer, 'Graduation.' He then looks at me and, in front of my daughter and her best friend, asks me, 'And who are you going to fuck?'"

"Again, wow." It was all she had to say.

"I told him how inappropriate that was and listened to his tirade about how proper we Southerners were. I just kept thinking, *Four more days and I. Am. Gone.*"

"How did you pull it off?"

"I told my sister, Kim, and my friends Kelly and Deanne about the advice the attorney gave. I called the girls' dad, Mike, which was a very painful call to make, and told him that I was leaving Bill and that he needed to take Caroline for the summer until I could make arrangements.

"Then I contracted with a moving company and put them on notice for June 1. That was the date Bill had a Turner Broadcasting event in Atlanta, so I knew he would be gone a good four hours. That's when we planned it all. Kim, came to help and brought her sister-in-law, and my friend Deanne also came. When we were almost finished, Kim looked at me and asked if this was all I was taking. Then she started packing up my prized antique French cabinet. I told her I didn't have permission to take that; she smiled and looked at me and said, 'Well, either you take it or you-know-who will have it for sale on her Facebook page.' Funny, both my attorney and my sister were right. I am so glad she made me take the cabinet. I still cherish it today."

"So you didn't get much in the divorce?"

"Oh, I got a lot that day; I got my freedom and my life back." I was sad as I thought back on the memory, but I continued. "We had a 7,000-square-foot house decorated to the nines, and I took one small U-Haul truck, two SUVs, and my car full of things. But that's what they were, just *things.*"

She looked at her watch, and I knew our time was up. As I walked out into that sunny June day, I thought about the other day in June when I left life as I knew it and never looked back. How much had changed in three years. I moved to Atlanta, struggled to find my way back into the workforce after having been gone for so long. I eventually took a position in marketing and PR with a group of luxury magazines, which should have been a great start to a newfound life. But instead, I found myself driving into my garage, closing the door, and leaving the car running when I desperately thought things were never going to change.

But they did.

Chapter 30
Like a Prayer

With age comes clarity, not wisdom. I thought about this as I looked through my closet and tried to decide what to wear. So many choices crammed into this walk-in. So many memories tied to a certain dress, or shoes, or jewelry. Maybe that's why I can't seem to part with any of my wardrobe. Each represents a part of who I am, who I was, who I wanted to be. And like my memories, I pack these items up and carry them with me each time I find myself needing to leave.

Yet, I don't let go of the past, I just repurpose it. Like the Cynthia Steffe outfit I had chosen to wear that day. It's a two-piece cotton skirt and lace-up top with a miniature floral print on a black background. It is not who I am at all, now. *But maybe who I am supposed to be?* I originally wore this outfit when Bill and I were in L.A. for a shoot before the Oscars. We were in La Perla— I'm still not quite sure why the CNN producers chose this location to film— and I thought this outfit was perfect. My black La Perla lace bra peeped ever so tastefully from the lace-up cotton print. Cheryl Tiegs, the first American supermodel, was in the store—incognito in her laid-back California style, yet

I still recognized her as she slipped out into the street so as not to interrupt the filming. I felt so Southern in this outfit, like someone who was going to a church social, while Cheryl was casually chic in jeans and a simple white tee in trendy L.A. I wanted to be like that, but it was never who I was. I was never comfortable being casual. I grew up always having to dress appropriately for every occasion—always having to "dress the part," whatever that may be. Always having to choose who I was going to be each day, and that day I wanted to be anyone but me.

"My mother said something to me recently that really shocked me," I began today's session, taking my seat and adjusting my skirt below my knees.

"That doesn't sound like the mother you describe to me," she said.

"I know, which is why this incident took me by surprise. We were sitting at the kitchen table having lunch after church. She had fixed a roast, some rice, and her green bean casserole. A 'Sunday supper,' if you will. Daddy and I were talking about Jennifer, as we often find ourselves doing after church, when Mother said she didn't believe in the power of prayer.

"I almost fell out of my padded Parsons chair. She and Daddy brought us up in the church: First Baptist of Jonesboro, then First Christian. We went to Sunday school and church on Sunday morning *and* Sunday evening. Choir practice and Bible study on Wednesday nights. We were in youth groups and hosted church parties at our house. We were the definition of a 'God-fearing, churchgoing, Christian family.' And here my 80-year-old mother has confessed to me and Daddy that she doesn't believe in prayer anymore."

"Why did she say that?" Dr. H asked.

"She said that she prayed for Jennifer all of her life, and in the end her prayers were never answered. That Jennifer never straightened out, never overcame her addictions, never lived a life free from drugs or alcohol, never got to see her boys grow up. So she didn't believe in prayer anymore."

"What was your response?" Dr. H asked me as she lit the beach candle.

"I told her that God *did* answer her prayer, but not in the way she wanted. I surprised myself. But I have been reading a daily devotional by a popular preacher. He reminds us that God has a plan for our lives, and it might not be in our time frame, but we have to be patient. I told her that maybe God's plan was to take Jennifer to heaven to release her from her addictions, from her pain, from her burdens here on earth. I think that was His answer to my mother's prayer.

"Jennifer took her life on August 9, 2005. It was a Tuesday, but we didn't find out about her death until the next day. Wednesday was (and is) Bridge Day in my mother's world, which means no one bothers to call her or try to schedule anything between the hours of nine a.m. and four p.m. So it was very unusual for Mother to call me just before she left for bridge that day.

"I was in my bedroom, standing just in front of the 'lipstick' couch that was in front of mine and Bill's bed. I answered my cell phone immediately when I saw it was her. She told me she had just gotten off the phone with my nephew, Luke. He is Jennifer's oldest son, and he had been living with me since the boys were taken from Jennifer due to her drug use. Luke was a freshman in college at UGA, over 18, and therefore he was going back and forth from my house to his old house since he was an 'adult' and no longer bound by the court, which had said Jennifer couldn't see her children until she could pass a drug test." I used my fingers to quote the word *adult*. I encouraged him to go see his mother; I knew she needed to see her children. And they needed to see her, despite what the courts said.

"Anyway, she asked me to call Luke, she said he sounded strange when she talked to him. So I called his cell. I don't know how to describe it, but his voice was very slow and low and weak. You could tell there was something terribly wrong, so I understood why Mother asked me to check on him.

"I asked him if he was OK, if everything was OK, and then he told me: 'Mom is dead.' I don't know what sort of sound I made, but it must have been a primal scream because Bill came running into the bedroom as I dropped to my knees on the Oriental rug in my perfectly pulled together bedroom. My brother-in-law, Jim, must have taken the phone from Luke, because the next voice I heard was his, asking me to let my parents know.

"Jim had come home from work around six p.m. that Tuesday, and he found her in the hallway, hanging from the attic. Then Luke, who had left my house to go to his mother's around three p.m. the next day . . ." I trailed off as I tried to remember. It is one of only a few times when my memory does not serve me well.

"When I found this out, I was so glad it was Jim who found her and not Luke. Luke's cell phone was on my account, and I remember opening the bill the month after her death. It was when the phone companies still sent bills that listed every call. I saw that Jennifer had called Luke's cell that day. But Luke being Luke, he decided to go to the bookstore before heading home. He didn't have his phone on him; he had left it in the car. He is a very intelligent kid. He was so wrapped up in the books that he didn't know she was reaching out to him. I often wonder, had he headed straight to her house, would he have found her?

"By the time he got to the house, Jim had already found her. He had cut her down, and she was lying on the floor of the hallway. I guess they called the police, who in turn called in the Georgia Bureau of Investigation—protocol for a suspected suicide. I find it odd that neither Jim nor Luke let us know about her death that night. Why didn't they call us? I have never asked either of them that question.

"No one knows how one will react to such tragedy," Dr. H explained. "But it is strange that they didn't let anyone know."

"It wasn't until I got to Mother and Daddy's house that morning that I found out she had hung herself. After I called Daddy, Daddy called Mother and told her to come home, that something had happened to Jennifer. Then he called Jim, and that's when Jim told him what she had done.

"Everyone, including me, assumed she had overdosed. So imagine our surprise at finding out she had jumped out of the attic? And then when we discovered she had superglued her hands together. . ."

I pause, take a sip of my water, and gladly take the tissue she offers as I try to hold back my tears.

"Jennifer researched different ways to kill herself, I am guessing since her browser history showed searches for Kurt Cobain and others. One of the articles she read was about how a person automatically tries to 'save themselves' when they try death by hanging. Apparently, it's a natural reaction to use your hands to grab the rope around your neck . . . anyway, the 'solution' to this was to superglue your hands together so you couldn't. And this has comforted me, in some strange way."

"How?" she asked.

"Because it made me realize that she must have really wanted to die . . . she was determined to succeed in the death of her addiction. And this was the only way to be free.

"There's a book by Kevin Hines, one of the few survivors of suicide by jumping off the Golden Gate Bridge in San Francisco. He talks about how the very moment when he jumped, his first thought was to reach back and try to save himself. I often wonder if Jennifer had those thoughts when she jumped? Or was she finally at peace? How long did she hang there in the hallway? I don't know how long you survive when you fall—do you?"

"I'm sure it varies," she said quietly. "I don't think you need to worry about the details; they would be too painful if you knew the nuances."

"I guess you're right; my fucked-up mind would just keep playing them over and over in my head until it burst. That's how I feel now, going back and reliving all these 'adventures' of my fucked-up life."

"I don't think it's a bad thing, Lisa." She sat up in her chair and looked directly into my tear-filled eyes. "From all I have gathered, you were a walking time bomb; there was no telling how much more you could take before you imploded. And that's exactly what happened, remember? That's why you are here. It is by retelling these moments that you are able to acknowledge them and put them behind you. You can open the closet, pull back the rug, and release all these secrets you have forced yourself to keep."

"I guess you're right. It's funny, because I always thought of Jennifer as the strong one. And I still do in the sense of the courage and the strength it took for her, or anyone, to take their own life. But maybe, just maybe, I am strong too?

"You are stronger than you give yourself credit for."

"I've always hidden behind my looks. It was the easy way out. I should have been a scientist; that's what I really wanted to do. But I became a writer, a journalist instead. I could have faded into the background of intelligence where looks didn't matter. Instead, I relished the power of opening doors with just a smile.

"Is that how you view yourself? As just a pretty girl?"

"No. But it is how everyone else sees me, so why fight it? Maybe that's the point my mother finally got to. Maybe that's why she doesn't believe in prayer anymore.

"I remember one night when I was really tired; it was almost six months after my suicide attempt, and I was struggling with the boss from hell at my job at the magazine. I had recently put in my notice and put my faith out there to be able to keep paying my bills. I got angry at God. I was crying in my apartment that I shared with my daughter. I got down on my knees, looked up at the ceiling, and literally screamed through my tears: 'What do you want from me? I am tired and hungry and have been working so hard and for what? I am lonely. I am asking you to send me someone. Someone I can love and who will love and cherish me.'"

"So you questioned God's plan?" she asked.

"Very loudly," I said.

"What happened?"

"I met NS the very next day."

Chapter 31
Pearls Before Swine

"In fact, I met NS when I was on a date with someone else," I explained. "A dear friend, Meg, who is also in PR, kept telling me that a client of hers really wanted to go out with me, and he insisted she set up a date. It was December 2012, almost two years since my divorce from Bill, and other than the torrid 'relationship' I had with a former pro soccer player, I hadn't been on a date of any kind."

"What do you mean by torrid relationship?" she asked.

"It was shortly after I moved in with Lydia in Atlanta, and I met a guy who was ten years younger than me. He was a former pro soccer player, very handsome, but not the sharpest knife in the drawer, as my Uncle Jake would say. He and I went out a couple times, but we were really only fuck-buddies, you know, 'friends with benefits' kind of thing. I think he was in love with me, but he was really bothered by our age difference, plus he wanted children, so there was that. It only lasted a few months; I think I used him as an excuse not to date."

"That makes sense," she said. "It was a kind of insulation to the predicament you found yourself in at the time."

"Exactly," I agreed. "Anyway, I eventually acquiesced to Meg's request and agreed to meet up with her doctor client, but on my condition that it be just prior to an event I was going to, so that I could 'escape' if needed. She said all he wanted to do was have a drink with me, to get to know me better. Nothing else."

"And did you? Need the excuse to escape?"

"Definitely," I told her, emphasizing my words. "It was exactly as I predicted. I met the doctor at six p.m. at a very popular restaurant at a mall in Buckhead. I chose to meet him there because it was directly above the store where my event was to take place at seven p.m.

"We met at the bar, and I ordered my usual: champagne. He talked about how much he had been wanting to meet me and go out with me ever since he saw me at an event earlier that year. Then he proceeded to tell me about his place in Las Vegas and how he was going there for the holidays, and he wanted me to go with him."

"So it wasn't just to meet for one drink." she stated.

"No, it wasn't. I politely declined his invitation; then I looked at my watch, which was really just ornamental, and told him thanks for the drink but that I had to get to my event that I was co-hosting. It was just all too much, too fast for me. In hindsight, maybe he was the answer to my prayer? But in true form, I ran from the right guy and into the arms of a swine.

"And that's when I met him. I was walking out of the restaurant when I saw him, sitting in the atrium area eating dinner. I recognized him immediately as the owner. So I walked up to him and re-introduced myself."

"Had you met him before?"

"Yes, but it had been about eight years earlier, maybe a little less. I had met him at another event. I was with Bill at the time—we had just moved back to Atlanta—and we were attending an Atlanta Press Club meeting. One of Bill's old friends introduced us. He was with his mistress at the time, and everyone knew him as a player. I saw him a few years later at a charity event. That time he was with his wife."

"So you knew going in that he had a reputation as a player, yet you still went out with him?"

"Yes, I did. I wasn't looking for love or anything really. We just organically met and found out we had this chemistry. It's really as simple as that."

She nodded her head as if to say she believed me.

"NS put his arm around my waist and his hand on my hip; that's when he noticed I wasn't wearing panties, I came to find out later. Which is why he was very interested in getting to know me better. He gave me his cell phone number and told me to call him the next time I was in town. Turns out, I was meeting a girlfriend for drinks the very next day, and she suggested we go to a particular place. So I texted, and when I arrived, he was there. He bought my friend and I a drink, and when she left, he sat down with me and we had dinner. That was on Wednesday, 12-12-12."

"Interesting," she said. "Do numbers mean anything to you?"

"Not really, I just find it entertaining the sequence of events of our meeting. We spent Christmas evening together; he bought me a black lace nightgown, which should have been my first red flag. He flew me down to his second home on New Year's Day, and we went deep sea fishing. In the interim, he bought me shoes and clothes. And everything was going nicely, until it didn't."

"What do you mean by that?" she inquired.

"What I mean is that he wined and dined me and bought me gifts—and all the time, he was still married: separated, but married with a girlfriend-fiancée I didn't know about."

"Love bombing," she sighed, then let me continue.

"I know, I should have *run*."

"How did you find out about the other women?"

"That's the worst part. People had told me about the other woman, but he kept insisting that they were not together, that he wasn't engaged. Then the Saturday before Valentine's, we go out to dinner with his brother and his sister-in-law, who were living with him. I can only imagine what they must have thought about him and all the women he had in his life."

"So you think you weren't the only one?"

"No. I'm not so naive to think that what he did with me behind her back was the only time he did this to her. Anyway, we had a lovely dinner at another restaurant, then headed back to his house. I was planning on my spending the night, as was he. I was in the living room when he got a call, which he left the room to take. He then comes back into the room with a very odd expression on his face.

"He then tells me, in a nervous voice, that I have to leave. His girlfriend had called him to let him know she didn't have her children that night and that she was on her way over. He was beside himself, trying his best to get me to leave. I was furious and embarrassed; he told me to tell his brother that I had to leave suddenly."

"And what did you do?"

"I grabbed my purse and coat and headed out the door, telling him that he could lie to them. Then I got into my Jag and drove home. I was so upset. I went home and went to bed and didn't speak to him again."

"But you must have; I mean you are still with him, correct?"

I went into detail on how he always wins me back. He brought me flowers on Valentine's and left them on my doorstep. Pink roses . . . I'm not particularly fond of pink roses. I prefer white roses. I revealed to her the tale of my roller-coaster relationship with him, and I left with the same feeling I have when I know my mother is disappointed in the choices I make.

Chapter 32

Friends in Low Places

It was the dead of summer, and I had been reluctant to keep up my appearances of sanity with my friends, family, and my own personal Freud. Everyone knew that I was going down a path of self-destruction with NS, but I couldn't help myself. I was caught in a triangulation and trauma bond that would only become more apparent as my time with him kept going. I say "more apparent," but not to me; however, it was to all of those around me. I had stopped going to see Dr. H regularly, and many of my sporadic appointments were canceled because he asked me to cancel. He also made me throw away the medicine she had me on; he didn't approve of medicine.

I was wearing a black and white Michael Kors 'scuba' dress—pretty appropriate since I felt as if I were drowning with no life preservers in sight. My friends were so disappointed that I was seeing this "horrible" man that they told me as much. They called me to warn me that he has a reputation for stalking women when they break up with him. He's rumored to have a girl in all parts of Atlanta that he handles with the precision of a circus acrobat. He is a narcissistic sociopath, which I would learn on my own in the cruelest way. But at that point, I was caught up in him and couldn't seem to find my way back to normal.

"You're late," Dr. H looked at her watch. *Why is it that everyone automatically looks at their watch as if to confirm the obvious? It's very Pavlovian in its nature*, I think, but then think better than to make matters worse by bringing up the subject. I was late. I was late because I had snuck off to see him when everyone thought we were done, over, finished. Problem is, when two sex addicts collide, it's very hard to give each other up.

"Yes, I am," I replied.

"No excuse, no apology?" she asked.

"No excuse. I am just late."

"You are rarely ever late anymore, and never by almost thirty minutes."

"It's twenty-six to be exact," I said. "And I was notoriously late all my life."

I knew she knew why I wasn't here on time. We had been discussing my weakness for NS for the last two sessions. She had the same opinion that everyone in my circle, and out of my circle for that matter, had: "He's a liar, cheater, textbook player, and he will never be faithful to anyone. Not his wife, whom he is still married to and currently divorcing. Not his longtime girlfriend, or "fiancée," who left her husband and lifestyle for him. And not me: the one who walked into this spiderweb and got stuck in its silk trappings even after finding out about who he is and all of the other women he has entrapped.

"I was with him," I admitted. "I know what you're going to say."

"And what is that?" she asked.

"That he is toxic and everything he touches becomes toxic. That I am very fragile and have been doing so well not seeing him, not buying into his lies and broken promises and empty dreams.

"That it sets me back every time I give in and see him, and that it is never going to change. Like Einstein is said to have explained, 'the definition of insanity is doing the same thing over and over again and expecting different results.' But I prefer Edgar Allen Poe's version, who said, 'I became insane, with long intervals of horrible sanity.'"

"Is that what you think? That you're insane, and when you have moments of sanity that's when you can't cope?"

"Something to that effect, yes," I replied.

"Even your demeanor is different when you come back from one of these weak breaks. It takes me longer to reach you, to make you see how good things are going for you. Then you fall back into his spell, and I feel as if we take major steps backward." She was disappointed; I could hear it in her voice.

"I know. I can't stop. I think I can handle it, but then I get all 'girly' and start to have these stupid emotions. I try to pretend it's only sex, but I love him. That's why it's so damn good. I love him, the way he loves me and takes me to my happy place time and time again, over and over."

"You know what you are describing is an addictive behavior toward the act of sex?"

"According to whom?" I challenged her. "I know you are trying to point out that I am a very sexual being because of my past, that my early abuse and feeling special about the attention is why I have this craving for sex. Why I love to make love. But it's different with him. It really is the most incredible high for us both."

I looked at her and realized I just made her point. I referred to sex as an "incredible high." I knew I had lost the argument.

"Your time is up," she said in that disappointed tone of voice, like the one a GPS computer uses when it says "recalculating." "I think we should try to have you come in again later this afternoon or first thing in the morning. I don't want you to think this behavior is acceptable. I'm sure you have had to lie to your family and friends again, and I know how that hurts you. Remember what you told me about the time your good friend Pam texted you to call her?

"That she had a terrible dream about you? And that you had secretly flown down to the beach to see him and her dream was that you were still seeing him and lying to everyone. And, that you came to her in a dream sobbing asking for help to stop. You have to remember how many of the people around you who love you do not want you to continue to see this man. There must be a reason. Please go home and seriously think about what that reason is, and let's schedule another appointment for tomorrow."

I picked up my purse, the Louis Vuitton that he gave me, and I took a look at what I was wearing: Burberry raincoat, Jimmy Choo black patent leather pumps, and a black and white Michael Kors dress. All from him. And I remembered the reason I still saw him. He's good with materialistic and emotional blackmail. And I fall for it every time. Everything else is smoke, lies, and alibis.

Chapter 33
Nowhere to Go but Up

"I want to apologize for yesterday," I began.

I was back to apologize, but also because I was feeling out of control. Gone was my all-black cotton attire I originally picked out to wear that day. I was in all white: a very Marilyn Monroe-style halter dress, but in a summer gauze material, with clear Manolo Blahniks and a quilted Chanel bag. I was wearing the color of surrender.

She was sitting on the couch next to me but said nothing. I noticed something I missed the day before: she had gained weight. I now know she was not pregnant, only retaining water. It reminded me of a sketch from Bill's TV show that I saw years before I met and married him. It was about a drive-thru funeral home. In the episode, the actors were discussing their dear departed loved one, who was a big girl and retained water. The line goes: "She also retained Ding Dongs and Old Milwaukee." Or something like that.

I thought about how he called my daughter fat and how he treated her differently because of her weight. I guessed it was my turn to talk.

"I know how destructive that relationship was—and is—and like the addiction it is, I have to be strong enough to resist. He is never going to be faithful to anyone; he is still married, engaged to a woman who is more of a mother figure to him, as were most of his wives, which means he will also need a 'bad girl' to satisfy his sexual desires. That's what I was supposed to be—someone to please him. Turns out he thought he fell in love with me, yet he was obligated to another woman, not his wife, who left her life for him. How fucked up is this whole thing?"

"Are you still seeing him?" she asked.

"Yes and no," I replied.

"That isn't an answer."

"Technically," I said, "it is."

"Either you are seeing him, or you are not. And by 'seeing' him, I mean having sexual relations with him."

"Then, yes," I said, "I am 'seeing' him."

"This is not good for your mental health, and you know it better than anyone."

"I keep telling myself that I am going to stop. After Valentine's Day, or after Easter, or after his divorce court date, or after my birthday."

"You're delaying the obvious," she said.

"And that is?"

"The pain that you must go through, once again. You—and by *you*, I mean both of you—keep hanging on. Neither of you can quit each other. He has no reason to. He has his cake and is eating it too. It's *you* who is compromising. *You* who sits home alone on major holidays. *You* who is the secret mistress that waits by the phone for his availability." She was showing her anger.

"I'm not sitting by the phone," I said, not even convincing myself. "I go on dates. I go on trips."

"You will never be free of him until you totally block him from your life."

"He's still paying for my apartment. So when the lease is up I am going to block him." She wasn't buying my excuses.

"You know your sister will help you out. You have told me how much she despises him; how you ran to her and cried in her arms time and again when he has left you behind to go out and live his life as it suits his needs. So the rent is just an excuse."

"My whole life is an excuse," I confessed. "I don't know how to stop." And then I started to cry. "I'm having a bad day," I said through tears.

"You are having a weak moment. But you have proven over these past few months how strong you can be. Look into the mirror; see yourself as others do."

"I wish I could, but I just don't understand. If I am so smart, beautiful, charming, and witty, why do I fall victim to these types of men? Why did they choose me?"

"*Because* you are smart, beautiful, charming, and witty. They prey on what they lack in their own selves," she answered.

"I am tired of being a victim," I said in defense. "That's why I haven't let him destroy me without a fight. I remember the first time he left me to go to her. We had just returned from an amazing trip to San Francisco and the wine country. We got back on Thursday night, and I was preparing to be with him on Friday when he said he couldn't see me that weekend; it was 'her weekend.' That was only three months into our relationship and the moment I found out about her." I took a sip of water and gulped it down hard as I remembered.

"How did you respond?" she asked.

"I was numb. I was supposed to meet my dear friend AB at Cherokee Town Club for cocktails. I called her and asked if I could come to her house instead. I went in, told her what happened, and then stood in her kitchen and cried on her shoulder."

"Did you say anything else?"

"No, she simply let me cry. She poured me a glass of wine and told n. could stay with her as long as I needed to."

"And how long did you stay?" she was giving me her look of disapproval. "I stayed the weekend. Well, until Scott came back."

"I don't know Scott, is he new?"

"No, Scott was the guy I was seeing when I met NS. We dated off and on for a year. Or whenever he was in town and in between his 'catting' around."

"You know how to find them, don't you?" She took note of this.

"No, Scott was not like that. We had a great friendship and intellectual curiosity about each other. We understood each other. We even shared the same birthdate. Both Geminis. We would talk and then make love. Fall asleep, have breakfast." I laughed out loud at a memory of Scott.

"What did you remember?" She was getting to know me very well.

"I remember one time, it was a very romantic evening. We went to dinner. Came back to his fabulous place in Buckhead. It was summer and he had Cristal champagne chilled for me. He is the only man who ever bought Cristal for me. We sat outside on his balcony, sipping champagne, when he excused himself. Next thing I know, he comes back, takes me by the hand and leads me inside the bedroom to the bath. He has the entire bathroom lit with candles and has drawn a bubble bath for me. It was probably one of the most romantic nights I have ever spent."

"And why did you stop seeing him for NS?" She had a strange look on her face, as if trying to understand.

"I don't know. Maybe we are better friends. He told me our timing was off, that we can't seem to be single at the same time. I will say after that night, I was confused about Scott. The next morning, we watched Wimbledon in bed. Drank our coffee. He had something to do, and so did I. We were getting ready, and I was about to put on my lipstick, when all of a sudden I turned to him, lipstick in hand, and said, 'Would you like a blow job before I put on my lipstick?'"

233

..1

acted surprised.

of course he smiled that big smile of his and well you ..st." I smiled. "We still talk about that. He says it is one of his r ten favorite memories. That and the text I sent him the weekend I spent at AB's house getting over NS."

"And that text said?

"Are you in town? I need a revenge fuck."

"And?"

"And he was out of town at a wedding. So no revenge fuck that weekend." I looked at my watch, which never keeps time.

"I'll say it again. You need to realize how strong you are." She was emphatic in her tone.

I didn't know what else to say to her. I knew what she was saying was true. But I was weak and tired, and I am an emotional cutter. I fought the urge to flee her office. I didn't tell her that I had had thoughts of suicide once again. I didn't tell her I was not sleeping, or that I could barely make myself get out of bed in the morning. I didn't tell her NS made me stop taking my Prozac because he doesn't believe in taking pills. Or, maybe because he didn't like the fact that to be with him I needed an antidepressant. I didn't tell her my secrets. I reverted back to my safe ways and kept quiet, but inside my mind was reeling. *I am small again. I am not strong. I am not a survivor. I want to take the easy way out. I can't do this on my own. Or if I can, I do not want to. There is something deep inside of me that doesn't want to be the perfect child anymore. I don't want to understand. I don't want to take the high road. I don't want to play by the rules. It's like my daughter once asked me, referencing her sister, when she was 5 years old: "Why is it I play by the rules, and she has all the fun?"*

I am a good friend, good mother, good sister, and a good daughter. What else am I supposed to be? I am not a good partner, because I can't seem to find the right guy to share my life with. All my friends are right; I am not allowed to pick my next husband. If there is even going to be one.

I am alone and I am tired and I don't want to have to put on lipstick. I want to run with scissors and jump off cliffs and eat the last piece of cake. The bar has been set too high, and I am tired of standing on my toes to reach it.

I finally spoke.

"I know I have to let go of him. I know it's for the best—for me and for him and for everyone touched by the lie that is our relationship. It's just . . . I don't want to be alone. And yet, with him I am always alone."

"Then what are you afraid of?" she asked, looking deep into my green eyes, trying to make an impact.

"I don't know. I guess, more than anything, I don't want to end up alone."

"But you just said so yourself: With him you are alone. Does that once-a-day phone call he sneaks away to make to you really make that much difference? Does the occasional text message matter?"

"It does to my heart," I answered truthfully.

"You need to stop listening to your heart and let that big brain of yours have a say in this matter."

We were done for the day. I smiled through my tears. I got up and left her office to make my way back to my one-bedroom apartment in the heart of Buckhead that someone else is paying for; alone with only my thoughts and a bottle of champagne to keep me company.

Chapter 34
After a While

Strength is measured against weakness in most situations—an arbitrary emotion that plays off one's sense of well-being. I had been going through my emotions and uncovering long-forgotten truths in hopes of becoming stronger, but mostly my reward for looking under the iceberg had been sleepless nights and anxious days covered in self-doubt I didn't even know I possessed.

Perhaps I had made a breakthrough, for I felt stronger on this day. I was dressed in my go-to uniform: short black dress, black high heels, and compact black purse. All designer, of course. It's my holy trinity of fashion, and it always had the ability to empower me. I was wearing some of the jewelry Mother had given to me, understated but elegant, just like her. I was ready for this session, , so I took my seat and asked Dr. H if I could read my chosen words out loud. I recite the poem, "Come the Dawn", by Veronica Shoffstall.

"This is one of my most trusted poems," I said after I finished. "I read it over and over again when I was divorcing the girls' father. It comforted me when nothing else could."

"Yes," Dr. H said. "It's one of mine as well. But how does it make you feel now?"

I find this a strange question since I am feeling strength in my words and actions and assumed she would have noticed.

"They comfort me," I explained. "In a way it's a very beautiful way to say 'grow up.' I remember when Mike and I were living together, my mother, who did not approve of my living arrangement, came over one day to see our home and my new engagement ring he had just given me. She was not one to hide her feelings when her children were doing something of which she disapproved. When I asked her if she liked my ring and the fact that I was getting married, she said, and I quote: 'Well it's much better than your present living situation.'

"When my eyes started to well up, she added: 'Goodness gracious, Lisa, by the time I was your age I had borne three children and buried two.' That's strength."

"Your mother lost two children before you?" she asked.

"She lost two boys. Then came Jennifer, then me, then Kim. I grew up always thinking I was the middle child, but I was more like the first born in terms of achievement, honors, etc. Then after Jennifer died, Kim and I realized that we had been counting wrong."

"What do you mean? In what way were you counting wrong?" she asked.

"Jennifer was always in trouble; always the one who did exactly what she wanted to do, more like the baby of the family. Kim always felt left out, like the typical middle child. And I was more like the first born—the overachiever who could do no wrong.

"And then it hit us, Jennifer would have been the baby had Glen and the other boy survived. So our new made-up birth order made sense, to us anyway. I was more like the 'Type A' first born, Kim more like the misunderstood middle child, and Jennifer like the coddled baby who was always in trouble."

"Do you put that much stock into the birth order or any other astrological symbols? You seem way too intelligent to believe in such things." Dr. H was amused at my assessment.

"I actually do. I believe in miracles and signs from above and that when we are born and in what order can determine our path in life.

"I remember when Bill and I first moved to Woodstock, New York, from the city. And by city I mean New York City. I totally did not fit in. I had found a niche in NYC from a fashion/PR standpoint, but clearly my Southern Baptist upbringing had in no way prepared me for the Jewish entertainment community, which influenced the liberal north that was New York. I had felt a kindred spirit with these beliefs much more than with the redneck, right-winged South I left behind.

"But in Woodstock, I found it a bit crazy that these people would burn sage in a room to 'cleanse' it before a new person came into a salon for a haircut. They would wrap their hair in burlap for who knows what reason and wear clothes that looked like they were crafted by the villain in *Silence of the Lambs*.

"I remember one day I was preparing for a very important meeting of the key players of the Woodstock Film Festival. I was chairing a committee—planning the film parties and opening and closing events. The meeting had been planned for weeks, but on the morning of the afternoon on which it was to be held, I got a call from the festival office. They were canceling the meeting because, and I quote: 'Mercury is in retrograde.'

"Of course, I was shocked and immediately Googled the term. I laughed about it then and several times after. But start to think about the times when your best-laid plans did not go as you expected, and I assure you will find that Mercury is, indeed, in retrograde."

"So do you believe in witches and unicorns too?"

"And Santa Claus," I added.

"I'm sorry if I seem callous to your revelations; it's that you strike me as someone with a high level of intelligence who would not entertain the common notions of astrology." She seemed to be backing down.

"I am a person of high intelligence and one who bel
science based on proofs. But as I've told you many times be
which is the sign of the twins, so there are really two of
you. I believe deeply that there is a God, and he has show
many ways. Whether or not I have listened to him or chosen the right path is
my own free will and my problem. I may or may not be here now because of
some bad decisions. But I truly believe that it was not my time to go, which
was why Lydia was home the night I attempted suicide—she was supposed to
be at her dad's.

"I know I was meant for something greater. I think, as a survivor, it is my
path to tell my story, to let others know that it's not their fault when abuse
happens. I think I've shared this with you before, but I often wonder if I am a
very sexual person because I was sexually abused as a child, or if I was abused
because I am a very sexual person?" I also wondered if I was repeating myself.

"You know you can't be sexual at the age of four. It is not something someone that young has any knowledge of, let alone feeling upon which to act."
She was adamant in her statement. "It's not your fault, Lisa. None of this is
your fault." She closed her book and gave me a knowing smile, as if to say, *I'm
speaking from experience.*

As I said my goodbye and walked out into the light of day, I recited lines
from the poem "Comes the Dawn." And I wondered secretly how many times
my mother had to do the same.

Chapter 35
The Road Taken

Each road in life has an end. We graduate from our chosen tier of education and leave behind empty promises to always remember the friends we made along the way, only to go on to our next adventure and our next goodbye. The only "relationships" that we carry with us from year to year are with family—not our friends, nor our work colleagues, nor our husbands. We can graduate from school, leave our jobs, and divorce our spouses, but family is bound by blood—and reunions. I think of these things as I'm driving to my last appointment with Dr. H.

I am listening to "Dear John" by Taylor Swift on repeat…how can one so young capture my thoughts and experiences, and put them into a song, when it took me many more years to define my situations? I sing the lines about a chess game and think of the girls' dad.

I look down at the outfit I have chosen for today: a simple, fitted black knit Ralph Lauren dress, leather "harness" belt, and over-the-thigh black leather riding boots. I was dressed for battle. But if I was ready to ride out of town and into the sunset, then why was it so hard?

It had been three months since I had sat on her couch. I didn't know how to tell her that after our last session, when I went on about how this time with NS was going to be different, that he literally left me in Charleston to find my way back home, alone. We had an argument over something insignificant, which I found untenable, so he walked me to the nicest hotel in the city, paid for a room, and left me alone in the hotel. The next day, he abandoned me via the Concierge. He dropped off my suitcase there with an envelope that contained a rent check, cash, and a note saying to find my way back to Atlanta. When I heard the knock on my hotel room door, I thought it was him…but instead it was the bellman delivering my possessions and instructions to go home. So I did. I flew to Atlanta, then I flew down to the beach house where we were living together and packed up all my things, so when he went back to the house, all traces of me would be gone.

Taylor is now telling me what I already know: I should have run as fast as I can.

If only I had listened to my friends, my sister, myself. To Taylor…

"My mother's best friend died last night," I began what was to be my last session with Dr. H.

"I'm sorry," Dr. H said in a genuine tone.

"She was the wife of the man who molested me when I was four years old," I added.

Dr. H just nodded, then asked: "And how does this make you feel?"

"It makes me feel like a long, dark chapter of my life can finally close," I answered. "You know, I never told my mother or father about the molestation. And I don't think his wife ever knew… that was our dirty little secret. When he died, it died with him. I was about to turn sixteen when *he* passed away; he had promised he would get me a car for my birthday."

She waited for me to finish my thoughts, but she was looking at me in disbelief.

"I've been holding this in for so many years, and now I wonder if the molestation was really what defined me, or did I use it as my excuse all of these years?"

"Don't you think you should have told someone?"

"I did. I told Jennifer. He molested her, too."

"I don't know what to say," Dr. H replied. "It seems like your entire family is good at keeping secrets. But I am curious if you think you really would have been a different person? Is this your crutch? And now that your mother's friend has passed, maybe you feel like you don't have any more excuses not to confront the woman you have grown into?" she asked.

"You mean the trophy?" I asked as I adjusted my dress over my boots.

"Are you still thinking of yourself as an object?"

"No, but you *know* I have been seen as one. Unfortunately, I didn't realize it until now."

"And why is that?"

"I'm not sure…I always thought I brought more to the table than just looks. But I am not going to let this opinion cast upon me by others define me. I do not want to be one of those women who marries an older man for his money, is put on a shelf, taken out once in a while to be admired, and then put back in its place."

"Is that your definition of a 'trophy wife'?" she asked.

"I think it is the perfect definition. I think it is *the* definition. I have been running away from that title most of my life. I am so much more than an object; I am not meant to be put in a corner, on a shelf, behind glass, and only brought out when my rightful owner decides it's time. I am too smart to play that game. And that's been my problem all along. I need more, I want more, and I keep searching for more, but I always end up with someone who wants to keep me closed off from the world. In fact, my sister Kim has been telling me this for years; she says I put so much of myself into my husbands' careers instead of focusing on my own. It's like when I am alone, I take care of my needs, but when I am with a man, I can't just let him take care of me…I still try to contribute, to work; besides, they never live up to my expectations."

I pondered whether to tell her that not only has NS left me yet again, but he is trying to come back. I decided to keep this tidbit of information to myself.

"That's the breakthrough I have been hoping for," she said. "But it saddens me that you still liken yourself to an object."

"I know. It came to me as I was going through my boxes at Mother and Daddy's house," I said.

Ever since I left Bill, my life had been packed up—scattered from my parents' house to my sister's basement, to my apartment, and to storage units in between. My life—broken into pieces, wrapped in paper, placed in cardboard boxes, waiting to be opened, assembled, and put back together.

"I found my favorite doll from my childhood," I told Dr. H.

I thought I had lost her in one of my many moves. But I opened this old dusty box, and there she was. Her white and green dress was now faded, her shoes were missing, and her hair was unkempt. But I looked at her face, into her eyes, and I remembered who she used to be…who I used to be . . . and I felt like I found myself again. It was as if I were that little girl—still full of hope, and dreams, and wonderment.

"And now with my mother's best friend gone . . . well, things have come into focus."

"How so?"

"Daddy was telling me and Kim a story after church one day; he said that I always seemed to get what I wanted when I was little. It was like the sun followed me. He reminisced about the time we were at the beach at a restaurant. There was a gum ball machine, but instead of gum, it with filled with clear oval balls containing different prizes. I looked at the machine and pointed to a ring with a green plastic stone and announced that was the prize I wanted…

He gave me the nickel, or whatever money I needed, and sure enough, when the prize came out it was the exact ring I had chosen."

"What does this mean to you now?" Dr. H asked.

"It means that, like Dorothy, I had the power all along. It is within me. It's within us all. We have the power to ask for what we want and to believe that we deserve it, and then it will happen. I think now it's called 'manifesting'," I said with a nervous laugh.

"I had forgotten who I used to be before all these terrible things happened to me. I was so intent on bending to the wants and needs of the men in my life that I let go of that little girl who believed in goodness and happiness, who took her prized dolls down off the shelf and played with them…not to leave them stuck up there to be admired, untouched. But to actually take them down to be loved.

"I discovered that you can be in a crowded room and still be lonely. If you are outgoing, friendly, funny, and love being around people, yet are not allowed to be any of those things once you are taken out in public, then what's the point?

"And that's what I mean when I say my shelf life as a trophy wife is up. I don't want to have someone else determine my wants, my needs, my worth… to tell me how beautiful I am and charming I am, and then put me back on the shelf to wither away, gathering dust—all alone. What was it Proust said about possession? 'Desire makes everything blossom; possession makes everything wither and fade'?

"Well, that's what I was to each of my husbands…I became a possession left to wither and fade, until I summoned the courage to leave."

"You remember who you are, who you were meant to be," she commented.

"Exactly! There were always glimpses of my former self that would emerge once I left a bad marriage. But I would fall in love with love again and always run into the arms of the wrong man. I think they saw my vulnerability, sought me out, and preyed on my weaknesses.

"Weaknesses like my inability to give up, my eagerness to please, and my apologizing for the sake of ending an argument. These weak men are the ones who sought *me* out and put me on a shelf. Knowing that, more than anything, I wanted to be free to be me, which made them fight harder to keep me all to themselves.

"And now how do you feel?" she asked.

"I feel vindicated. I can look back on the roads I have traveled to get here and realize I might not have taken the right one each time, but it was the right road for me *at* that time. I choose to believe everything happens for a reason. I chose to be that little girl who could pick the perfect prize out of a big glass bowl, and play with her dolls, and run with scissors; the little girl who was followed by the sun...

"I choose to embrace the woman I have become but remember the girl who suffered in silence to get me here.

"And here is where I will begin, again. Unburdened by my past, learning to live and to love, not as if I am a prized possession, but as a person."

"Do you think you have changed? Have healed?" Dr. H looks up from her notebook.

"I don't think one ever truly heals from childhood wounds. They haunt you like a bad dream. You know the one where you're alone in the woods and something is chasing you, but you don't know what or why? The dream that you make yourself wake up from? I think that's what you have to do. You have to choose to wake up, to forgive, to be happy. What's the saying, 'If you want to be happy, then be'? I could choose to dwell on all the horrible things that have happened to me. I could go through life medicated, just existing. But I make a conscious effort to be happy. It's ok to visit Self Pity City, every once in a while; you just can't stay there. So, no I don't think I have changed, or healed . . . I have chosen to be happy. To forgive myself."

"And your biggest regret?" "I now believe that my biggest regret was losing myself in my husbands' lives and not building one for myself. My dreams were put on hold…and my desire to be the 'perfect wife' led to the demise of my career and the breakdown of my marriages…

"But I am ok with my brokenness," I say, then ponder for a moment. "My brokenness is a part of the whole of who I am. It is my brokenness that lets in the light, as I'm reminded of my favorite Carly Simon song. It lets me see the good in people, lets me give out spare change to those who congregate on street corners. The cracks may have healed, but luckily still remain as a reminder that although I may have been broken, I was able to put myself back together. Maybe that's why I have a hard time throwing away things that are broken: teacups, earrings, people…there is still beauty in their brokenness…

"In my little place I call home, you will find family photos displayed in sterling frames, broken tea cups of fine china, mended. And books. Lots of books. But in the corner of my living room is a birdcage with a beautiful green and golden sequined hummingbird; she dangles from the small hook in her gilded cage, and every so often, I see her move."

"What are you thinking?" Dr. H breaks my train of thought.

"I'm thinking about birds," I laugh. "And how in my home I am surrounded by birds. I have pictures of birds, sterling bird candlesticks, and small alabaster birds placed amongst my prized possessions of leather-bound books and cocktail table tomes, yet I never fully understood my fascination with birds…

That is, until I found an old photograph of me as an infant; swaddled in softness; an arm holds up my tiny frame and above me, attached to my crib, is a mobile of different species of birds….flying high above my world, unburdened and just out of my reach."

"And the arm holding you up?" Dr. H. asks.

"My mother's," I answer. "I always thought it might be my mother's insecurities that held me back, but I know better now. It was my own insecurity. In fact, I believe that my mother's blue-sky world in which she lives, in which she saw life—and still sees life—is what helped me to cope. She has been there all along, having my back, holding me up."

I handed her a slip of paper, a nod to how our sessions first began. It was a poem I wrote after my molester's wife, my mother's best friend, died. She read it out loud as I sat and let the tears flow slowly from my eyes:

There is a picture of Jennifer and me,

when she was five and I was three.

It brings me sadness since it was taken before,

I was molested at the age of four.

And she was as well, or so it seems,

So we coped in our nightmares when allowed to dream.

And I think to myself, who would we have turned out to be,

if we weren't molested after five and three?

It makes me wonder—would you have taken your life?

Would I have become a Trophy Wife?

Would you still be here, could we all grow old?

What would have been different, if only we had told?

She folded the paper and handed me a tissue, clearly moved by my words.

"It's not that I gave up on my career, or my marriages, or myself," I explained. "It was just easier to pretend things didn't happen. And when forced to look at my life, it was easier to let go. But when I tried to let go, God had other plans."

She simply nodded, then asked, "Now what?"

"Who knows," I said. "Maybe I'll take my sister Kim's advice."

"And what is that?"

"Quit chasing dick and write a book."

So, here I am…a writer once again.

The End

Epilogue

I open my eyes only to realize I am flat on my back on the floor of my Watercolor home in the exclusive 30A enclave of Florida's Gulf Coast. I slowly reach up with my left hand and touch my left ear; it is bleeding. I am bleeding.

The pain in my neck and ear is so palpable that I can only concentrate on the pain. My head is literally spinning from what I will later learn is a concussion along with a severe neck sprain caused by a closed-fisted punch to my neck that was so powerful it knocked me off my feet and unconscious onto the floor. Those dark mahogany-stained planks of the finest wood— meant to absorb the comings and goings of those invited into the life we began together almost four years ago—now absorb my tears as they silently fall.

My left arm is numb, as is my mind, and I can't really feel anything even though I am still holding my ear, cradling it. I am on the floor by the fireplace, the one I so lovingly decorated with pictures of our lives entangled and autographed books by famous authors; it now holds up candles ensconced in decorative lanterns meant to figuratively light the way back home.

I look to my left and see the Heidi Daus-designed teardrop stone earring of moss green I'd been wearing. It matches my dress, matches my eyes, and now is on the floor about six inches from my head . . . smashed and damaged and on its back, just like me.

I turn my head and look up to see my husband standing over me. His eyes are wild as if he is looking straight through me, as if I wasn't there, as if he didn't want me there.

I am crying in disbelief as I slowly begin to realize what happened. I am still on the floor as I watch him turn around and walk up the stairs to our bedroom, leaving me discarded where I lay like one of his dishcloths dropped in haste, not worth bending over, picking up, and placing back on the counter.

He doesn't bend down and cradle me in his arms to tell me he is sorry, to beg me for forgiveness. There is no attempt to help me up, no words to inquire if I am OK. I think of these things as I lie there in our home, alone and injured.

I eventually find the wherewithal to slowly make my way up off the floor. Using the fireplace to brace my moves, I begin to understand the severity of my injury. I am dizzy and off-balance, and my left arm is numb. But it is the pain in my head and my neck that fuel me to do what I do next.

I find my phone and capture my image and the time, 10:21 on 10-22-20. It pains me to look back at this photo. Of the tears staining my cheeks, the hollowness of my eyes. My hair appears wet; I wear the disbelief of a victim coming to terms with the truth. It is now my truth, and I make a split-second decision on where I go from here.

I pack up my car, escape to my neighbor's house, and begin a new journey—on my own.

Acknowledgements

Where do I begin? —Which happens to be my mother's favorite Andy Williams song...so I will begin there. To my Mother, Grace, who gave me life, the love of books and the joy of shopping, all of which I still have to this day ... and to my father Richard, who gave me his green eyes, quick wit and uncanny math skills, which were never put to good use. This book is a product of both my parents, Richard and Grace Rayner, as am I. Together they brought the three of us girls up into a loving, religious, fun and exciting home...it is through no fault of their own that we turned out like we did. They simply did the best they could with what life gave them—three very different children who grew up to cope in their own way. To Jennifer, who left us broken when at the age of 45, died by suicide...and to my sister Kimberly, who as the youngest, was witness to all of our circumstances... and who stayed to pick up the pieces. It is Kim who believed in me and in Shelf Life enough to invest in its reality. Without her love and support, *Shelf Life of a Trophy Wife* would never have made it onto a bookshelf.

Of course there are my daughters: Lydia Grace, who literally saved my life, and Caroline who gave me two grandchildren and with that, learned to love me again. Both have been, at times, my biggest cheerleaders and my deepest critics. Together we celebrate all things cerebral, the love of music, books and Champagne.

To my family members who read my early manuscript and encouraged me to continue with Shelf Life—my fabulous Aunt Gail Marsden Hutchins, and cousins Terry Marsden Brasfield, Rebekah Brasfield and Laura Hutchins Dove.

To my running mates, Ellen Harden Ward and Kimberly Salter—I still think of that day and how you both were there to help mend my brokenness.

A special thank you to Jack Watts, my fellow writer and friend who brought me to the Fitting Words table.

I wouldn't be here without my publisher/advocate: Dan Wright of Fitting Words—who as a former publishing executive with Thomas Nelson (the largest Christian Publishing company in the world) overlooked the 31 F%@Ks in Shelf Life and believed in my message strongly enough to accept my manuscript. Also, to Kate Eute—my amazing editor who not only corrected my mistakes but also sent me words of encouragement along the way. To Jennifer, Fitting Words' proofreader, who brought the edits to completion. PS. I kept in "ennui" ….

Also, my first official editor and dear friend Stephanie Davis Smith, who told me one day after editing my manuscript, "I know several people that only one if the things that happened to you has happened to them, and they are all on medication and in bed…" You have been an integral part of this journey! And to Amy Burton Storey, my very own story advisor!

My therapists over the years: Angie, Joyce, Elizabeth and Cindy…who were all rolled into Dr. H.

A huge shoutout to Vikki Locke, who was my first reader and who encouraged me to finish Shelf Life "for everyone's sake". Also, Jennifer Brett, Meg Reggie, the aforementioned Stephanie Davis Smith, as well as Rob Bennett, Brandy Walker Hodge, Marian Goldberg, Michaeline Roland, Elissa Rosen, Rivka Tadger, Kelly Norris Wagstaff, and Kelly Willett—your initial response to my manuscript and belief in me and my words meant the world to me.

For my Fellow Trophy Wives, a big thank you for being a loving community of amazing women: Dottie Smith, Cathleen Smith, Joanne Chessler Gross, Pam Smart, Merry Carlos, Melanie Boltax, Nadia Chochol, Jane Dean, Lisa Fuller, Cathy Thrift, Brittany Duncan, PL Dickey, Jada Loveless, Michelle Edwards, Su So-Longman, Dawn Worthy, Corinna Allen Cook, and Beth Davidson Carroll.

To Laura Turner Seydel, although technically not a Trophy Wife, she is a Trophy Friend who has always championed me!

Also, my legal eagles: Ken Nugent- my personal (injury) attorney and my greatest defender; also James Morton, and Todd Christensen.

My Modern Luxury ladies and friends who helped me navigate my re-entry into the working world: D'anne Cagle Heckert, Carris Fairfax, Jana Graf, Lacee Watkins, Hayden Pascal, et. al. Also, to Michael Dickey.

MY Glam Squad: Photographer Lachen Boufiji, Hairstylist CJ Nicotera, Make-up artist Sarie Mateo Gray and a special shoutout to Tom Abrams and Britt Wood, who always choose Fabulous!

A special shout out to Jason Bunin—whose fashion print was the inspiration for the cover.

To my UGA/KD Sorority Sisters: Jean Koening Story, Nancy Farrah Dunlap, Jan Youmans Collier, Beth Martin Mangum Smith, Anne Wolfe Sapp, Diane Brown Vaughn, and Vikki Slauson Vincent, Beth Harrington Brown, Chrissie James Thead, Leslie Laird— you all helped me through a very tough time…even though you never knew.

To my *Writing Sisters* and NY Pitch Cheering Section: Alicia Blando, Melissa deSa, Joani Elliott, Robyn Fisher, Kate Jackson, Pia Kealey, Delphine Ladesma, Marti Mattia, Victoria Sams and Grishma Shah. I have enjoyed this journey with y'all!

And my LK Rayner team: Lydia Martin Church, Caroline Hines, Stefanie Lister Wardrep, and Abigail Watts. WE did it!

To Jennifer Brett aka Mrs. Parker who always told me, quoting Oscar Wilde of course, 'Be yourself; everyone else is already taken.'

To my favorite ex-husband, Bill Tush, whose charismatic personality and presence in our lives provided a window into an enchanting world for a time that we will forever be grateful for.

Lastly, To Kim—again, thankful that we share the same DNA, that we are sisters but especially thankful that we are friends.